BUILT BY THE SPIRIT

J A C K   H A Y F O R D

BUILT BY THE SPIRIT

J A C K   H A Y F O R D

Regal

A Division of Gospel Light
Ventura, California, U.S.A.

Published by Regal Books
A Division of Gospel Light
Ventura, California, U.S.A.
Printed in U.S.A.

Originally published as *Rebuilding the Real You.*

Cover Design by Barbara Levan Fisher
Interior Design by Britt Rocchio
Edited by Ron Durham and Karen Kaufman

Library of Congress Cataloging-in-Publication Data
Hayford, Jack W.
    [Rebuilding the real you]
    Built by the Spirit / Jack Hayford.
        p.   cm.
    Originally published: Rebuilding the real you. Ventura, Calif.
    Regal Books, c1986
    Includes bibliographical references.
    ISBN 0-8307-1922-9 (pbk.)
    1. Men—Religious life. 2. Bible. O.T. Nehemiah—Devotional literature. 3. Christian life. 4. Hayford,
Jack W. I. Title.
    BV4528.2H38 1997   97-18343
    248.4—dc21   CIP

1 2 3 4 5 6 7 8 9 10 11 12 13 14 15 16 17 / 05 04 03 02 01 00 99 98 97

Rights for publishing this book in other languages are contracted by Gospel Literature International
(GLINT). GLINT also provides technical help for the adaptation, translation and publishing of Bible
study resources and books in scores of languages worldwide. For further information, contact
GLINT, P.O. Box 4060, Ontario, CA 91761-1003, U.S.A., or the publisher.

CONTENTS

PART THREE
SUSTAINING THE CITADEL

FOR YOU, SIR!

This book is about a guy named Nehemiah and how he helped a whole lot of other guys do two things: (1) get *their individual lives* together in a way that positively affected the future for themselves and their families; and, (2) get *themselves corporately* together to achieve a goal that radically changed the future of their nation.

Not bad!

So you can see why I was excited when my publisher suggested I write a special edition of my study on the book of Nehemiah, especially prepared for men! The result is this book of tools for building a man's life in partnership with the Holy Spirit.

"Nehemiah!?" you ask. "Can anything good come from here!?"

On the face of it, this small book, buried at the end of the historical books in the Old Testament and filled with a lot of apparently unnecessary lists of names and who-did-what-in-the-project details, doesn't exactly seem to "crack" with excitement. But that understandable question might be answered with another one: Nazareth!? Can anything good come from there!?

That's what a disciple-to-be named Nathaniel said when he was told that Jesus might be the Messiah, and told the name of His hometown. But Nathaniel found out the answer to that one! And I think anyone wondering about Nehemiah will also be surprised with his or her discoveries.

So, Sir—I'm inviting you to take a look...and then, dig in.

> **And by the way, Ladies...**
> Although I have adapted this book specifically for men, you too can benefit from Nehemiah's principles.
>
> Women often ask, "What does God's man really look like and how can I partner with the man in my life to help him become all that God fashioned him to be?"

Nehemiah provides the blueprint that may prove useful
for both of you to look at.

For more than 10 years, my book, *Rebuilding the Real You*, has
found solid acceptance and use by thousands of believers—as they have
discovered keys to *partnering with the Holy Spirit for personal development and growth*. The idea of retooling this book to address the distinct needs of men caught my attention for special reasons.

First, because as you might know, I'm seriously involved with the
whole movement of God among men today. Many of us have met at
stadiums across the nation. Others of us have become friends through
the privilege I have of broadcasting on nationwide radio and television. In short, men are an assigned priority on my agenda: assigned by
God.

More than 25 years have passed since an icy Illinois morning when
I was trudging through some woods near the banks of the Mississippi
River where I heard a Voice whisper to me: *Begin to meet with the
men of your congregation*. Elsewhere, I've told the story of my
response—and how it has affected the shaping of the entire life of the
congregation I have now served for more than 28 years. I know what
great things can happen when men grow in God's grace—and build
with His Spirit!

Second, I was given a "key" which I have been privileged to share
around the world. I don't mean I'm the only person on earth who
understands the book of Nehemiah—that would be ridiculous, to say
the least!! But I do know that the insights I gained from this book
about building have become remarkably useful to literally millions.

By means of books, study guides, audio and videocassettes and
national broadcast media over two Christian networks (CBN and TBN),
these studies have gone forth for decades. It is humbling to encounter
people everywhere I go, who say, "Studying your material on Nehemiah
changed my life!"

Today, millions of men are hearing the voice of God in the midst of
an awakening—God is calling His sons to rise. You and I are two of that
number, and I'm hoping you'll join me for the journey. My discovery
of the wealth in Nehemiah's pages has changed my own life, and it can
change yours, too.

The good news is that you can partner with the same Holy Spirit who gave us the book of Nehemiah. He's ready to give depth of insight and richness of experience to every man who asks for it. And you can count on Him to not only rebuild your broken places, but also to bring growth to barren ones. He's a Builder!

Let's partner in building with the Spirit!

Jack Hayford
Van Nuys, California
Spring 1997

PART ONE

PERIMETERS OF POSSIBILITY

Jerusalem's walls now dashed, destroyed
and smashed beyond belief,
Display the pain of wounded people, burned
and gashed by grief.

But comes a Helper, One who sees within
those shattered parts,
A citadel of strength and joy, rebuilt
from broken hearts
He loves and treasures.

—J.W.H.

CHAPTER ONE

As a Man Among Men

The Word:

Jeremiah 29:11 (TLB)

For I know the plans I have for you, says the Lord. They are plans for good and not for evil, to give you a future and a hope.

The Target:

- An awakening is occurring among men, and in that atmosphere we are invited to a partnership.
- To accept is to move beyond the limits of humanly devised self-help plans that inevitably fail where life's most important issues are involved.
- Nehemiah not only points to a partnership with the Holy Spirit, but it also points to a pattern of partnership for each of us as "a man among men."
- Basic "starting place" issues of "faith" help us zero in on the path forward.

As a Man Among Men

As I scanned the Blaisdell Arena in Honolulu, my heart was as full as the next guy's. It was 10 days into the New Year and the place was packed with thousands of men rising to praise Jesus Christ at the national kickoff event for Promise Keepers. The gathering was powerful...stirring!

Praise songs soared. Cheering men thundered out their declarations of the worthiness of Christ the King—the Lord of glory. Even though the time was nearly 9:30 P.M., the place was still electric when I was introduced. The crowd had risen as one in their positive response to Coach Bill McCartney's challenge as he set forth the PK thrust for the year ahead. Then hundreds of men responded to the gospel as Mike Silva proclaimed Jesus' saving-delivering power. Now I was up to bat.

I never get used to this privilege. As often as I've opened God's Word before a stadium full of men, each time is a fresh miracle for me. Each setting is a fresh moment ready to explode with the possibilities that the Father's almightiness can bring. So many times, guys have asked me, "Jack, what does it feel like to speak to 60,000 men?"

I always answer, "I'm never speaking to the crowd: I'm just talking to one guy. Just one." I feel that way right now.

This book is designed to let me speak to *you*. To make a way for the two of us to talk, as you join me in saying, "God, I want to invite You to build me into a better man among men." The operative word here is "invite"—to welcome help—to allow Him, the Almighty One who made us, to show us how to become the man we each want to be.

This book is also a means for us to *dig into God's Word—together*. As men "among other men" we acknowledge our need for each other as well as our desire to strengthen each other. And Nehemiah is a dynamic case of men joining hands with God and with one another—entering a partnership with the Holy Spirit in order to discover the way He can build men into strong sons of the Living God.

The Holy Spirit has an awesome ability to *bring it all together*, and you're probably ready to admit your need of Him if serious "building" is going to take place. In one way or another, I have to believe you're the same as I: My *own* plans have had a way of backfiring, my *own* strength has usually been inadequate (especially where *godly* purposes have been involved), and my *own mess* has too often been the result. As somebody said, "A self-made man is usually an example of poor craftsmanship!"

We've all had our nightmare experiences with "doing it ourselves." Every family has horror stories with humorous punch lines—retelling the times they dug up the yard, tore out the wall, unplugged the sink, tried to replace the toilet, blew up the engine, overpruned the apple tree or cut the cat's claws and were almost killed doing it! So it's clear to us both that if the building of a godly life is what we are after, we're going to need to move beyond the limits of "self help." Nehemiah—a book of facts about a time of frustration—opens before us.

This is a book about the ultimate Helper, and about how God's Master plan for manhood can be recovered and realized with His help.

This is no wild-eyed claim. We have all learned to be suspicious of any book, tape or video that promises the moon—claiming to produce magical wonders through a new set of rules or a studlike body through a new set of exercise equipment. Infomercials sell the latest gadget or promote the hottest trend that will supposedly lead us to the top rung of whatever ladder we want to climb.

Quick-sell promises exploit our human fascination with the notion that more personality improvement, physical exercise, financial pyramiding, beauty and grooming, leisure and play or sex and sexuality will somehow make our lives "work." But this kind of "more" always ends up "less," because every program of human enterprise inevitably promises more than it can ever provide—that is, if we're looking for *real answers to building a life.*

Real answers call for a hard-nosed approach, then. I'm asking you to come alongside as we stride past the "quick sell" and the "cheap buy," because *living, workable answers* to fully realized manhood aren't there. Like a meat-and-potatoes kind of guy said about the latest puffed cereal: "I'd just as soon go outside at night, open my mouth and let the moon shine in!"

Any book, tape or video offering an angle on life that promises to change us "for the better forever" without the Ultimate Helper is bound to miss it. We need more than just "us," because while neither of us may be all that bad, we're not really good enough. When you start with man, human insufficiency is all you're going to get.

Sure, I know the proposition still survives today: "Man has what it takes. The inevitable realization of evolution's goal is within reach—a little more education, a little help, a little push, and we'll be there" (wherever "there" is). But when we arrive at the conclusions of human-based self-help programs, the results are always the same: We're muttering the classic Charlie Brownism, "How come we keep losing when we're so sincere?"

THERE HAS TO BE SOMETHING MORE

Still, brother, I *am* fully convinced that some marvelously incredible possibilities *do* exist in us as men—in you...as a man! My doubts about human potential only relate to our attempts at cultivating it without our Creator's partnership. But it is clearly reasonable to me that if the image of God was originally stamped on our human being, something very substantial, mighty and glorious is still there. Whatever damage may have been done in the meantime through human "sin in general" (by others) or "sin in particular" (my own), the fumbles and failures of the race or by my own rebellion do not put limits on what God Almighty can do.

This book is about discovering those possibilities for you, as a man among men. And the operative words are *among men.*

We're talking about partnership *with God,* but we're also talking about partnership *with other guys.* This shouldn't come as any surprise. God's coaching plan is built on making every one of us a team player:

- God called Moses, then teamed him with his brother Aaron, and Israel was delivered from Egypt.
- A dozen Israelis went into the Promised Land to check out the possibilities. But when the majority report "chickened out" on God's call to faith, Joshua and Caleb stood firm— as a team of God's men.
- David's reputation as a military genius ("he has killed tens of thousands!" see 1 Sam. 29:5) didn't dupe him into an

independent mode. He was strengthened by his profound, manly relationship with Jonathan.

And,

- Jesus caps this point: He trained His disciples in *groups*—first 12, then *70*—and then always sent them in pairs.

That wisdom is prevailing in today's men's movement. This isn't a privatized program of personal achievement for any of us. We're coming back to the Founder's fountainhead for grace, gain and growth. Men are learning that our greatest victories are not in self-achievement, but in becoming sold out to the idea of bringing glory to God "in the church"—that is, in the company and companionship of others who are committed to growing as disciples of Jesus their Lord and Savior (see Eph. 3:21).

That doesn't mean God doesn't also offer us personal and individual fulfillment. It just means that, as we'll find in studying God's truth in the book of Nehemiah, we all need the partnership and encouragement of fellow laborers as we set about *building with and being built by the Spirit of God.*

God is calling men to come out of the shadows of whatever their pasts may have held and to step into the light of His grace-workings today. It's our hour as men. And I believe a study of the men in Nehemiah's day as they worked on rebuilding the walls of Jerusalem can encourage our moving with that Spirit-directed trend. He is bringing men together so we can each "get it together!" As He calls us, He is also ready to help us. That's why we are repeatedly hearing of good things God is doing in the lives, homes, families and jobs of thousands of men.

God has graced us with a special demonstration of His readiness to *move among men* today. In the same way a man named Nehemiah came to lead and help men in rebuilding the walls of ancient Jerusalem, God has come to help us rebuild. This book in His eternal Word is intended to be a guidebook for us, showing how being involved with God's Spirit, as a man among other men, can bring not only glory to God—but also our greatest fulfillment personally as we discover His working in and through us.

The starting place is for each of us to come to terms with anything in, about or around us that is *broken*—whatever has been fouled up by accident, dented by disobedience, smashed by sin, ruined by rebellion or injured through ignorance.

We have all experienced something of brokenness: hearts, homes, health, finances, dreams, relationships. These wounds are as breakable as bones. They're equally curable, though harder to set. We may not all

THE STARTING PLACE IS FOR EACH OF US TO COME TO TERMS WITH ANYTHING...*BROKEN*—WHATEVER HAS BEEN FOULED UP BY ACCIDENT, DENTED BY DISOBEDIENCE, SMASHED BY SIN, RUINED BY REBELLION OR INJURED THROUGH IGNORANCE.

be basket cases, but it's certain we all need the Doctor. The Body needs the Great Physician, too. As a member of Christ's "Body," I want to urge you not only to join *me* as we search His Word for wisdom in rebuilding, but to seek out *other men*, too. Let's work through this material as teammates with other guys, so we can borrow "building skills" from each other.

OUR BASIC STARTING PLACE

As we get under way together, let me lay down some basic points that are my presumed starting place.

First, I believe the manly thing to do is to seek the real. That leads to the first article in my personal confession of faith: I believe that the ultimate, the consummate, the conclusive, the absolute, the final, the genuine—*the real*—is the Living God Almighty. He is larger than life and the Founder of all that life is meant to be.

I believe He is the Father of love and yet has the right to speak with authority to His children. He has given us His Word: His promises are real and His commands are to be taken seriously. Further, I've found He still whispers to the hearts of men in private moments. (He has to you!) And I believe that those whispers are best confirmed and seen to be authentic in the company of God's people, and that they will always result in aligning us more closely with His Word as revealed in the Bible.

I believe God sent the Messiah, and that He has proven the Messiah's miraculous capacity for meeting humanity's need by raising Him from the dead. Nothing could be more real than that, and when we stand together in the morning light of the reality of Jesus' resurrection, *nothing is impossible for your life or mine!*

One last thing.

I believe in *you.*

Despite all I've said, and will say, about the limits of our human resources, there are still some very strong things God wants us to believe about each other. First, I believe you care about your *becoming* the man God created you to become. If you didn't, I don't believe you would have read this far in this book. Second, based on what I have come to know through a lifetime of counseling with thousands in both intimate, private and personal sessions, I've learned the phenomenal twin facts of our *uniqueness* and our *unity* as human beings.

We're obviously unique: there isn't another you or me anywhere. But we're also remarkably alike—a unifying factor which has taught me that it is never presumptuous nor impersonal to speak to crowds—through a book, over the radio, by a cassette or via television. And amid our "samenesses" are two things: we **hope** and we **believe.**

You hope because we all do. Dreams are not rare; they fill all our hearts and occupy all our minds. God puts them there—that is, the ones that really count, and we each do, in fact, know which ones those are. Those longings, dreams, aspirations and goals are God-given. That's why He also breathes *hope* into our hearts to keep us targeted on the good and great things He wants to do if we'll enter into partnership with Him.

That's where "faith" comes in, and as I said, *I* believe that *you* believe. I'm not making a reckless proposition, because the Bible says that everyone has faith: "God has dealt to each one a measure of faith."[1] This verse doesn't mean that everyone's faith is perfect, accurate or functional. But it is there, waiting to be pointed in the right direction and applied in the right way.

Someone may say, "But I don't think I have faith," or, "I know someone who says they never had it, or they lost it." Still, I'm going to hold the ground of God's Word: He's given *each one* a measure of faith. I believe there is more than is known by most who doubt it. It takes a remarkable effort with a deep commitment to "not believe," for faith can rarely be crowded out of a human soul. Disaster may burn it, tragedy

---

AS THE SPIRIT IS AT WORK BUILDING TRUE MANHOOD IN YOU AND OTHERS, LIKE IRON STRIKING IRON, TOGETHER THE SPARKS CREATED BY INTERACTIVE CONTACT CAN SET THE HEART AFIRE WITH FAITH.

---

smash it, injury bruise it or arrogance denounce it. But faith, like seed buried under concrete, is difficult to keep down permanently.

Whatever your level of conviction about your quality or quantity of faith, we are en route together to seeing it nourished by being a man among other men. As the Spirit is at work building true manhood in you and others, like iron striking iron, together the sparks created by interactive contact can set the heart afire with faith. Jointly, we are headed toward becoming instruments of increasing grace under the Holy Spirit's touch, nourished by the truth of God's eternal Word and His risen Son.

One more thing: Join me in welcoming a new dimension of God's power into your life. Invite the Ultimate Helper alongside—His first name is "Holy" and He's the Spirit of God. He is as truly and completely God as either the Father or the Son. He is deeply personal, all powerful and ever present. And He wants to make Himself known in the details of your life and your relationships.

That He is one of the "Three in One," as the creeds put it, need not be a problem if such theological questions trouble you. He isn't running a heavenly quiz to see how much we know, for in the last analysis our salvation and our destiny will not be resolved by how much, but by *Whom* we know. I think your perspective about Him, about yourself and about other men will be broadened and deepened as you pursue these pages.

In Australia, the "Land Down Under," there's a kind of tree called the *jarrah*—sometimes called "ironwood." This tree is so heavy and dense and hard that termites hate it. Thus it isn't hard to figure out why the jarrah is so widely used in building—especially in the tropics, where termites abound. But let me tell you: It takes real strength and skill to build with jarrah. That's why I want us to see clearly our need of the Holy Spirit as we move into our study.

We're about to see how Nehemiah faced a heavy building project—one that depicts what God wants to do with you and me. Aspects of your life may cause you to wonder: *Is this a "jarrah" situation—one so hard I don't think I'll ever be able to "cut it"?*

Well, rest in this comfort—rather, *in the Comforter:* the Holy Spirit can handle it! Just as Nehemiah faced difficulty and opposition that seemed certain to block the completion of the building project he had come to lead—and never backed down but won—so the Lord is ready to work with us.

Let's go for it! We're a pair of men among the host of men God is "rebuilding" in our day. And we're about to see the pattern of possibilities that open up when the God of all grace comes as the Spirit of love and power to bring us unto His fullest and best—for His glory and for our fulfillment!

SPIRITUAL WORKOUT

1. What weakened or damaged areas in your personal life or family life could use some "rebuilding"?
2. What man or men in your life have been an inspiration to you?
3. Do you sometimes feel that you don't really need, or that you fear developing, close relationships or intimacy?
4. Even though you may feel the need for close relationships, are they difficult for you?
5. Do you think women generally make friends with each other more easily than men make male friends? Why?
6. Have you had any positive or negative experience with the current "men's movement"?

CHAPTER TWO

FINDING YOURSELF IN HISTORY

The Word:

Nehemiah 1:2

Hanani one of my brethren came with men from Judah; and I asked them concerning the Jews who had escaped, who had survived the captivity, and concerning Jerusalem.

The Target:

- To gain a grasp of the times, the place and the key peoples involved in the setting of the book of Nehemiah.
- To see in these the remarkable ways of God's sovereignty and the remarkable works of His fulfilled prophecy.
- To understand the embarrassing situation of the people, who had a temple of worship (relationship with God) but whose city was in ruins (no self-government).
- To be introduced to the first traits of Nehemiah's character, as he provides an introductory picture of the Holy Spirit's character as shown toward us.

Finding Yourself in History

The visit of a contingent of representatives from Jerusalem started it all. They arrived in Persia, not as a formal delegation but as a committee of concerned friends—and with that, the story begins to seethe with action. Suddenly, and with little preamble, the book of Nehemiah bursts upon the pages of Scripture as this dynamic story flows out of one of Israel's most tumultuous times in history.

Step into these pages: You'll probably find yourself here, as a man among men. The men we first meet will soon find—probably to their surprise—that in God's timing and purpose, they are poised on the edge of momentous historical events. To read is to wonder—at least at the beginning—if they had any real sense of the long-range destiny unfolding through them. Most likely not, because, as with all of us, most men are so occupied by the demands of life's daily duties that ordinary tasks preempt our higher expectations.

As for the men in Jerusalem, there was, of course, no way they could have known that in council chambers far away, matters concerning their future were beginning to take shape. But soon, their responses would be summoned, and their character would be tested by the offer of a possibility that they thought to be out of the question. As we begin to read about those events that would open a door of "hope beyond imagination" to them, let me urge you to begin *now*. Watch for yourself: Allow for the possibility that God has something of parallel significance for you too.

Picking up the book of Nehemiah, at once we are thrust into a convergence of events that requires review. We need to familiarize ourselves with the story's setting, not only to gain its "sense," but so we can also begin to see ourselves in its lessons.

Nehemiah begins his record describing a private conversation between himself and a relative from Jerusalem named Hanani who had just arrived in Susa (Shushan), the ancient capital of the Persian Empire. The mention of his inquiry "concerning the Jews who had escaped"[1]

brings us to the necessary beginning point of our historical study:
What Jews?
What captivity?
What escape?

A HISTORICAL SKETCH

To get a handle on all this, let's take five—a five-minute historical sketch of this adventurous season in Jewish history. So, step back with me to a century when the sovereign workings of God's Spirit brought into concert the activities of a half dozen kings, a spate of prophets and a displaced nation. And in the midst of it, don't be surprised to find yourself there as well!

The year is 446 B.C., and a full 90 years have transpired since one of the grandest moments in Jewish memory. Just under a century before, more than 50,000 Jews had been released by the edict of Cyrus, ruler of the Medo-Persians. Through the leadership of a remarkable and dedicated man named Zerubbabel, they had returned to Jerusalem. To say "they" returned refers to the Jews as a people, for, in fact, very few of the contingent who returned had ever been there before. The returning exiles were actually the children and grandchildren of people who

---

STRONG MEN DON'T HAVE TO BURN DOWN THE TOWN
AND TRAMPLE THE CITIZENS TO DISPLAY THEIR
MASCULINE LEADERSHIP POTENTIAL.

---

had been taken captive during the conquest and ultimate destruction of Jerusalem by the renowned Nebuchadnezzar—dreaded monarch of ancient Babylon.

Consistent with the methods of conquerors in that era, Nebuchadnezzar had not only leveled and burned their capital city, but his troops did everything possible to totally break the spirit of their captives. Soldiers corralled the vanquished by the thousands, drove them like cattle, and herded them from their homeland to Babylon. Their transport to a distant culture was a means by which the victors hoped to permanently dissolve their victims' identity as a people and to smash their wills as individuals.

Let me digress a bit and contrast this worldly measure of power with the "new masculinity" I see emerging in the men's movement during our times. A contrast is coming into focus. The brand of leadership that Nebuchadnezzar employed isn't absent from our culture, it's just applied in different venues.

"Mastery" is still the compulsive style of the spirit of the world. But we are beginning to see—even in some contemporary corporate structures—that THE Master was right when He said that the most effective leaders are those who will be servants instead of lords. It's Jesus' style, of course, and He's called you and me to learn it. Unlike false views of macho maleness, He holds up the ideal that "whoever desires to become great among you shall be your servant."[2] The message: Strong men don't have to burn down the town and trample the citizens to display their masculine leadership potential. But back to our story.

Prior to this destruction of Jerusalem, and the actual exiling of those thousands of Jews, Nebuchadnezzar had earlier gained dominion over Judea and its capital city, Jerusalem. For a season of nearly 20 years, He had installed puppet kings to govern the area, to keep it both accountable to and taxable by him. But due to recurrent resistance and sporadic instances of political rebellion against his government, he finally determined to sack the city and exile any remaining prisoners to his capital in Babylon.

During the period of those puppet kings Jehoiakim and Zedekiah, God raised up the voice of Jeremiah the prophet, who relentlessly warned of certain judgment. A history of willful disregard for God's laws was bringing down the curtain on the glory days of Judea's past, and Jeremiah predicted a coming captivity that would cover a period of 70 years. However, he also promised hope—hope in the Name of the Lord God. For Jeremiah said that after this period of time, the exiled families would be released, and there would ultimately be a return to Jerusalem, as well as a restoration of their Temple and their worship of the Most High God.[3]

And it happened. Just like that.

GREAT PROPHECIES FULFILLED

As the 70 years of prophesied captivity was drawing toward its close, an amazing combination of international events began to weave together. No human plan could have choreographed it all, but true to the great prophecies by no less than four mighty preachers—Isaiah, Ezekiel, Zephaniah and Haggai—the resultant end was the legal release by a new political regime in Babylon. Any Jews who wished to return to Jerusalem were allowed to go. Cyrus, the new monarch, issues the edict, exactly according to *Isaiah's* prophecy—a forecast that is all the more phenomenal in that he is even *named* by the prophet more than two centuries before he was born!' *Ezekiel's* prophecy is also a part of this miraculous montage. He had lived with the people through their captive experience in the regions of Babylon, but before he died he foretold their return—saying a reconstruction of their Temple in Jerusalem would occur.

You guessed it: that happened too!

Ezra, the priest-historian, not only reported the return of the exiles, but elaborated the challenges they faced in rebuilding the Temple. And just as he describes the difficulties the new-temple builders encountered, we are also introduced to two more prophets. The overcoming of the Temple "project obstacles" was stimulated through the inspiration of the prophets *Zechariah* and *Haggai*.

In other words, in this swirl of prophetic and historic activity, God is at work restoring His people while nations and their kings unwittingly bow to the performance of His will. Consider it all:

- The balance of world power swung from Babylon to Persia, and with the fall of the majestic city at the hands of Darius, it would seem that the fate of the exiled Jews would be even more complicated as their control went into the hands of those who had conquered their conquerors.
- Nonetheless, their deliverance came right on schedule. In the year 536 B.C.—exactly 70 years after the first contingent of exiles had been transferred to Babylon—Cyrus ordered their release. So we come to answer our earlier questions: What Jews? What captivity? What escape?

We now see how Nehemiah's words, "the Jews who had escaped," refer to those who, by the Emperor Cyrus's decree, were allowed to return and to begin rebuilding their city and their nation. And as they did, the Jewish people would never be the same again. The impact of the Babylonian captivity on the Jews had one positive result: polytheism—the idolatrous worship of many gods—was forever expelled from their minds and habits. Henceforth, only the Lord Jehovah would be their God forevermore, and Moses' words would resonate in their souls as they do in ours to the present: "Hear, O Israel: The Lord our God, the Lord is one!"[5]

Upon the return of the exiles, their primary focus was on a major undertaking—to rebuild the Temple in Jerusalem. Now, as a people for whom the pure worship of the one true God was their highest priority, the task was undertaken. That part of their story is in the small book of Ezra, which just precedes Nehemiah in our Bibles.[6] Ezra records this rebuilding project, which took 20 years from its inception until the Temple was completed, and then dedicated, in the year 516 B.C.[7]

God's promise of their return, and His promise of their Temple's restoration, had been fulfilled. The forgiveness for the past was evident in their return, and their restored relationship with the Lord was symbolized in the rebuilt Temple. But as the Jews would gather for joyous worship, one thing was still missing—one very crucial thing.

The walls of their city still lay in ruins.

THE JEWS' EMBARRASSMENT

Since the rebuilding of the Temple, two full generations had elapsed. As we open Nehemiah it is now 90 years later—90 years since the first families' return, and 70 years since their completion of the Temple. This is what is behind Nehemiah's concern, which centers on the fact that the city sits in embarrassment. The reproach reported to him is obvious to see.

Here is a people who have been able to reestablish their *worship*, but unable to secure their government. The missing evidence of a reestablished *rulership*—a respectable capital city rising above the ashes of its past destruction—is not forthcoming. Now, with nearly a century behind them since the first arrivals, and with more than 70 years elapsed since the rebuilding of their Temple, little excuse remains for so embarrassing a situation.

It isn't hard to imagine how readily and how justly surrounding peoples and nations might mock them: "Some God, Jehovah! What kind of glory can you attribute to a deity whose worshipers squat in humility before Him, but He unable to endow them with the ability to restore self-respecting government in their capital city!?" A restored temple of praise didn't seem to send many signals of testimony to the glory of a God whose people couldn't manage the "practicals" of life.

NEHEMIAH RESPONDS

This is what occasioned Nehemiah's deep grief and passionate concern. A city with a Temple, but with no walls or secured rule, was a blight on the name of its people and a reproach upon the name of their God. And it is this dilemma that drives Nehemiah to prayer—to compassionate weeping, joined to intercessory mourning and fasting.

Let's not miss this: The character of this man, who is introduced to us as a consultant or cupbearer[8] to the Persian emperor Artaxerxes, is profoundly evidenced by his willingness to care as he does. There is no reason for his concern in terms of his own situation. But his unselfish passion for the comfort and fulfillment of his people transcends his occupation with or protection of his own security, prestige or convenience. As we read, we will find Nehemiah:

- Interceding for the people (chapter 1);
- Risking his life for them (chapter 2);
- Seeking to secure their safety (chapter 4);
- Obligating himself in their interest (chapter 2);
- Unselfishly giving of his own resources (chapter 5); and
- Working to the complete the removal of their shame (chapter 6).

And with this, our historical sketch concludes, which has done much more than bring us into a meeting of the man Nehemiah himself, as well as an understanding of his times. We have also seen the emergence of a personality—a kind of person in the *history* of God's work with His people *then*, which magnificently prefigures something of *prophecy*—of God's ways of working with His people *now!* As we begin to see the man—the historic figure, Nehemiah—something of a picture of the Holy Spirit begins to become very recognizable. That is, if you've met Him!

Have you?

··

SPIRITUAL WORKOUT

1. Do you find yourself sensing that God has something special for you that seems blocked by circumstance, as with those in Jerusalem at the time of our study?

2. Can you think of an example in your own experience of a man who exercised either "servant leadership" or the false "masculine" leadership of raw power?

3. Do you ever find yourself inclining toward the Nebuchadnezzar brand of "rule by burning and binding" rather than the Jesus' way of "rule by serving and loving"?

4. Read Haggai 1:2-9 (a prophecy given at the time the people were 'giving up' on rebuilding the Temple) and answer these questions:

   a. Why did the people's work seem fruitless?

   b. Are you aware of areas in your own life in which you may be putting your own interests ahead of God's work?

   c. Do you ever feel that you are putting your hard-earned wages in "a bag with holes"? What measures might we take to remedy such a situation?

5. Have you, like the Jews deported from their homeland to Babylon, ever lived in a foreign country? Did the experience pose any difficulties for you, especially as a man? Have you ever found your character and commitment tested when traveling, or otherwise "away from home"?

CHAPTER THREE

Meeting a Forever Friend

The Word:

Nehemiah 1:1,2

The words of Nehemiah the son of Hachaliah. It came to pass in the month of Chislev, in the twentieth year, as I was in Shushan the citadel.

1 Corinthians 10:11 (TLB)

All these things happened to them as examples—as object lessons to us—to warn us against doing the same things; they were written down so that we could read about them and learn from them in these last days as the world nears its end.

The Target:

- To introduce key points of understanding about the Person of the Holy Spirit, His character, His concerns and His ways of working.
- To urge toward an acknowledgment of our need as men to move beyond the macho mentality to the wisdom of confessing our need of and dependency upon God's Spirit to help our weaknesses.
- To encourage a recognition of the distinction between being born of the Spirit and being filled with the Spirit, with appropriate action and prayer being expressed as a result.
- To note the similarities in the problems faced by the people of Jerusalem and those so many believers face today; how rebirth does not resolve all problems of past brokenness.
- To introduce the dramatic parallels that open up in the book of Nehemiah, between the name, character and ways of Nehemiah and the traits, character and ways of the Holy Spirit with us today.

Meeting a Forever Friend

Have you met the Holy Spirit?

If I were to ask, "Have you ever 'bumped into' the Holy Spirit?" the factual answer for every one of us would be yes. Because whether we may have recognized it or not, He has at one time—and usually, many more—in some way touched each of us. Still, even though we literally move through life among frequent encounters with His dealings in our interest, the Holy Spirit—Third Person of the Trinity (the Eternal Godhead, Father, Son and Holy Spirit)—tends to be somewhat of a mystery to most people.

For centuries He was referred to as "The Holy Ghost" (and still is in many places) and by reason of that designation—ghost—a dimension of unreality if not spookiness cloaks His person in many people's minds. This mystique of "unknowingness" or "ghostliness" has surrounded His Person for so long that far too few of us really know how to think about Him. But let's try.

To begin, the Holy Spirit is *personal*.

By personal I mean to emphasize that, like God—because the Holy Spirit *is* another expression for "God,"—He exists: *really, truly, actually, personally.* He is not to be thought of as some abstract force or as only a distant cosmic influence. He is *very* personal, and as one expression of the Three-In-One God who created us, the Holy Spirit loves us—loves *you!* He actively works to bring us unto the knowledge of Christ. He processes redemptive grace toward us, and He longs to bring us to full maturity in life and to the realization of His created purpose in each of us.

(*If the idea of the Trinity—that God is three persons in one person—boggles your mind, don't be surprised. It does everyone—even studied scholars and theologians. That ought to be expected too. In fact, I suspect we ought to assume the inevitable: if God is really as great as "the God above all" should be, our attempts to define the very richness of His essential being will transcend our best thinking, our whole human order and our entire grasp of things!*)

In His mission to reveal Father God to us, as well as to redeem us from our sin, Jesus shed a great deal of light on the personality of the Holy Spirit. He taught us that:

a. He is like Jesus Himself in character, temperament and works;[1]
b. His mission is to help us personally understand more and more about Jesus;[2] and
c. He has come to abide—to stay with us, somewhat of a heaven-given Forever Friend.[3]

The most cursory reading of John's Gospel, chapters 14 to 16, establishes these things: The Holy Spirit has been sent by the Father, in the Name of the Son, to *be with* each one of us and to *help us walk with* Him. There's nothing spooky about that!

THE HOLY SPIRIT ENTERS AT NEW BIRTH

The first thing to happen when a person comes to God the Father, and willingly receives the gift of life which comes through Jesus His Son, is that *the Holy Spirit enters that person's life.* Jesus described Him as a "Comforter"—literally, to define the Greek word *paracletos*—One who remains beside you to help, to counsel, to teach and to strengthen you.

His entry, though, is just the beginning. As surely as we open to His incoming through our receiving God's life-gift in Christ, we are also invited to open to His overflowing—continually. The apostle Paul told us to keep on being filled with the Spirit![4] And every sensitive and sensible believer in the Lord Jesus knows the difference between receiving the *presence* of the Holy Spirit, and walking in the *power* of the Holy Spirit. By both—His presence and power—He comes with a desire to increasingly expand the evidence of God's purposes in our lives.

The *fullness* of the Holy Spirit (see Acts 2:1-4), the *fruit* of the Holy Spirit (see Gal. 5:9), the *gifts* of the Holy Spirit (see 1 Cor. 12:28) and, most of all, the abundant, flowing *love* of the Holy Spirit (see Rom. 5:5) are all expressions of God's intentions in giving us His Spirit. In other words, to simply realize that the Holy Spirit entered when I received Christ is to grasp a precious truth. But you and also I need to

see more—to want more (i.e., "hunger and thirst for righteousness"—
Matt. 5:6).

The progressive and practical development of God's work in each of
our lives requires that we give a growing place to the Holy Spirit's
working within us. An old hymn says it well:

> O spread the tidings 'round,
> wherever man is found,
> Wherever human hearts
> and human woes abound;
> Let ev'ry Christian tongue
> proclaim the joyful sound:
> *The Comforter has come!*

The Comforter *has* come, indeed, and His mission is to help us
onward as growing sons or daughters of the Most High God.

An inspirational account of how this can happen is given by Pastor
Jack Deere, who candidly explained how for years he had taught that
the Holy Spirit's work was only through the Word of God. He did not
grant much place for an experience in the power of the Spirit, or a
daily role in His working *through* a believer's life, past the new birth.

Then British psychiatrist and Christian author Dr. John White
opened the Word of God to him, and Jack Deere testifies to how his
eyes and heart were opened as well. After a series of undeniable evi-
dences of the real and continuing power of the Spirit, Jack found himself solidly affirming both the need and the reality of the Spirit's ministry.

The Spirit of God has come to indwell, to fill and to overflow each
of us who welcome His working in our lives. And the best test of the
presence and the validity of the Holy Spirit's work in a believer's life is
shown clearly in the Word of God. He makes people more like Jesus—
more loving, more patient, more generous, more considerate, more
powerful in our service and more understanding in our attitude.

This chapter's "introduction" to the Holy Spirit we're pursuing right
now, which is kind of a *Holy Spirit 101 course,* is foundational to where
we're going in Nehemiah. Our fuller study will have a great deal more
to say about the Holy Spirit's work in our lives, so it's wise to see, from
the beginning, that our focus is *not to displace* Jesus with an emphasis

on the Holy Spirit, *but to replace* our weakness and personal inadequacy with the Holy Spirit's enabling presence. That's our objective: We want Jesus Christ to be "built into" the structures of our living—to be seen more fully in each of us. (Can you say a strong, *"Amen!"*?)

With that affirmation, we are probably at a good spot for me to pause and ask you quite frankly, my brother: As a man, would you say you are at a point in life where you are fully ready to admit your need of God's help—to acknowledge your limitations...your weakness? Let me tell you why I ask...

As men, we're all in the same boat in many regards. Among other things, we've all been sold a bill of goods; *a world-minded proposition that teaches us to believe that our strength as men is to try to prove our sufficiency as men.* With this come the tendencies—the habits— that do either of two things:

1. To *pretend*—that is, to try somehow to prove (to ourselves or others) that we've "got it together" (I'm "In control," and "Getting along fine on my own, thank you!"). Or,
2. To *depend*—that is, to rely on some other source of support than God (all the way from the *external*—money, clothes, brains, physical prowess, etc.—to the *maternal*— copping out through leaning on a woman who will "mother" me).

Beside the obvious illusions and self-delusions when we buy into the world-mind's propositions, we suffer worse for our *exclusions.* We end up leaving God, His Son, His Word and the power of His Spirit out of the essential agenda of our lives as men. The substitutes for the Spirit of God are always inadequate. That's why the wisest exertion of masculine courage is to acknowledge forthrightly—to *confess* my areas of weakness and need—to God first; then to other brothers as well. The next move is *to be bold enough to be humble*—to accept the help of the Spirit in dealing with it.

Even among people who have experienced the entry of the Holy Spirit into their lives—that is, people who have received God's love and forgiveness through Christ's death and resurrection—there are wide variations in response to the Holy Spirit. Too often a hesitation prevails, a slowness to allow the Holy Spirit "space" to work in their lives.

All of us are notorious for not asking God's help until our backs are against the wall. We humankind are persuaded that we can manage by ourselves, or else that to "bother" God for anything other than a crisis condition would somehow impinge upon His patience.

THE WISEST EXERTION OF MASCULINE COURAGE IS TO ACKNOWLEDGE FORTHRIGHTLY — TO *CONFESS* MY AREAS OF WEAKNESS AND NEED — TO GOD FIRST; THEN TO OTHER BROTHERS AS WELL.

This human habit of waiting until our circumstances are drastic usually means that by the time we finally open our lives to Christ, considerable damage has been done. The net result is that whatever our past, however gifted our capacity for survival, virtually all of us badly need the Holy Spirit's *restoring* work in our lives. It's the *Nehemiah story*, ready to happen with *us!*

- That work *begins* when He is welcomed.
- That work is *advanced* when He is permitted full reign.

*(If, by chance, you have read this far—but right now, you realize you have really never opened up to the **beginning** of God's Spirit working deeply and powerfully in you, your **first invitation** is to invite Jesus Christ, God's Son, into your life. Ask Him to be your Savior—for "there is no salvation in any other: there is no other name under heaven given among men by which we must be saved"⁵—only Jesus is "the Lamb of God who takes away the sin of the world"⁶).*

*(And if you **have already** received Christ, but have never asked Him to overflow your life with His Holy Spirit's power, your **second invitation** is to express that desire to Him: "Lord Jesus, rain the fullness of your Holy Spirit over my life." He will do that, for He is **both**, the Savior and the Baptizer with the Holy Spirit.⁷)*

THE HOLY SPIRIT DIRECTS GROWTH

Once we have begun our life in Christ, each of us will sooner or later be confronted with a crucial question: Will I learn to *live* by the same power that *birthed* me into this new life? Since the power that brought the life of Christ to me was by the Holy Spirit, what shall be the power by which I grow in this life? The answer is rather obvious: The same Spirit! But equally obvious is the fact that most of us are slow to draw on His enablement.

Paul wrote to the Galatians, "Having begun in the [lifepower of the] Spirit, are you now [by the energy of your own flesh] being made perfect?"[8] We all need the same reminder: New birth isn't the end of God's program for us. His Spirit has *started* something by His power that He wants to advance through our willing partnership to *continue* depending upon the same power.

The following is where the corner was turned for me—at least, in reference to the book of Nehemiah.

Dan had come to me. "Pastor," he said, "I think there's a lot of us who need some teaching from the Word on 'restoration.' Lots of us have been *saved,* we have opened to the *fullness of the Holy Spirit* and have *begun to learn a life of worship.*" He paused, thoughtfully, then continued.

"I don't know how to put it, but it seems like *lots of stuff has been broken in the past,* and while coming to Christ forgives that, there's still something needed—big time!—to get it all recovered: (pause)...Am I making sense, pastor?"

Well, I said yes—and I meant it. But I didn't know where to turn in addressing the subject the way I felt Dan's expressed need required. He was talking about a lot more than the "I need to grow" or "I want to grow" statement of a sincere believer. He was talking about how the path to that growth is so often cluttered with obstacles—hangovers from our private pasts—our past sinful lifestyles, our past lifetimes of wedged-in-place habits, our past bitterness-born-of-pain attitudes, or our past indulgences in sin which have left a horrific residue in our minds, our bodies—our physical, emotional, intellectual or spiritual systems.

- Forgiven we may be and forgiven we are.
- Reborn we may be and reborn we are.

But the inescapable, factual evidence of our pasts often trails us like a monstrous creature—an awful *present* reality that challenges the credibility of the *eternal* reality that has taken place in our souls. The remembrance of past sin is often inescapably present in some of its

WE MAY WELL HAVE BEEN FORGIVEN FOR THE FOOLISH SEEDS OF SIN SOWN "B.C."—BEFORE CHRIST CAME INTO OUR LIVES—BUT THE HARVEST OF THAT "SOWING TO THE FLESH" DOESN'T DISAPPEAR OVERNIGHT.

remaining fruit. We may well have been forgiven for the foolish seeds of sin sown "B.C."—before Christ came into our lives—but the harvest of that "sowing to the flesh" doesn't disappear overnight.

Of this we can be certain: God has forgiven it all! *"There is therefore now no condemnation to those who are in Christ Jesus."* That deserves a loud *"Hallelujah!!"* because this is the bright truth about our new God-given inheritance! But of equal, truthful certainty is the continuing presence of many personal problems bequeathed to us all from our pasts—at times even being the "trickle down" effect of things we were innocent of doing ourselves, but which have impacted our lives with drastic consequence. YES! Our salvation *does* solve the problem of our relationship with God. NO! It doesn't dissolve all the problems in our lives. New life in Christ *does* open the doorway to *solutions*, but only by walking through that door and patiently pursuing that way will those problems finally reach *resolution*.

This principle leaps out at us from the book of Nehemiah.

Within the pages of Nehemiah is the story of a people who had been given a new lease on life, but who were repeatedly blocked and shamed by their inability to demonstrate complete evidence of renewal. Their *rebirth* is seen in their return, but their recovery is unseen, and abundantly manifest in the rubbled mess called "Jerusalem."

As a people, they illustrate the incompleteness that often besets and bewilders reborn believers. Those Jerusalemites, frustrated by their inability to restore their capital city, depict believers who seem unable to regain control of life issues mangled in their pasts. Like those in ancient Judea, so often with us: recovery was so long in coming, the conviction grows that it is never going to happen.

But then something happened—No, *someone*.

Into this setting surrounded with despair, comes a man. Having heard of their distress from the land far distant where he lived, a kinsman named Nehemiah is *moved to action*. And it is in this regard—in the person of Nehemiah—that I began to see a mighty picture of the Holy Spirit at work in human experience:

- In the way that He comes to lead their rebuilding process;
- In the way he helps them recover walls of restored government, just as they have a temple of restored worship;
- In the way Jerusalem's *mess* became a testimony to God's *might*.

Here is a full color, pre-New Testament photograph of the Holy Spirit—the living, loving God who is as committed to our restoration as He is to our salvation!

I saw the picture when I noted how Nehemiah was sent by the king, just as the Holy Spirit has been sent to us by our King—the Lord Jesus.

I saw it by the way Nehemiah's work was essentially to lead, just as the Holy Spirit comes to show and grow us in The Way. Nehemiah didn't achieve the job *for* the people, but did it *with* them. He teaches them how to move forward in the rebuilding project, precisely in the same partnering way the Holy Spirit comes beside us to help.

I also saw the picture in the display of authority that Nehemiah brought to a downtrodden people; authority that engendered confidence; authority that cut effectively against those adverse to the rebuilding project. God's Spirit does that: He comes to extend the awesome rule of Christ in our lives—not only *to* us, but *through* us—against the dark powers of hell that oppose the Father's purpose.

As Nehemiah began to appear so clearly as a heaven-designed, advance photograph of the Holy Spirit at work in New Testament believers, I probed further in my study.

NEHEMIAH: THE CONSOLATION OF GOD

One of the most unforgettable moments in my use of Old Testament Hebrew language resources was the day I looked up the meaning of Nehemiah's name, which is as follows:

> Nehemiah: meaning, "the consolation of God"; derived from *nacham*—"to breathe strongly, to pity, to console"; and from *Yah*—"the sacred name of the Lord."

In short, I was stirred to laughter when I discovered it: Nehemiah means *"the consoling breath or Spirit of God"*!

Further background study revealed his name was built from a verb root that conveys the idea of *"pity which becomes active in the interest of another."* In it all, Nehemiah was not only beginning to appear as a picture of the Holy Spirit, but everything about this Old Testament character's name was precisely synonymous with His!

These first awakenings in discovering the availability of a profound study of the parallels in Nehemiah's role with the people in that day and the Holy Spirit's with us today opened to a further unfolding of this book of the Bible. Having been hardly prepared for the amazing discovery I made in the meaning of Nehemiah's name, I was all the more rejoiced with what opened in the Scriptures as I began to proceed with a deepening conviction.

At first I asked, Could it be that centuries before the coming of Christ—long before the gift of the Holy Spirit to the Church—that God Almighty had implanted in His own Word a coded message about the Holy Spirit's ministry of recovery? Could it be that forecast in this piece of Israel's history—in the same way as the ministry of Christ was prefigured in Old Testament events—that a message of salvation's fuller provisions was foreshadowed? Could it be that the historical person, Nehemiah, without realizing it himself, was living out a picture being filmed for all times? Are we viewing a photograph of God's Spirit assisting us in our weakness and the recovery of all those ruined parts of our lives that sin has disintegrated? Was it all happenstance? Coincidental?

The answer soon became obvious: Yes! No! *Yes*, God has put a glorious picture of the Holy Spirit's work in the book of Nehemiah, intending us to see how He would invite us to hope—and to partner with Him. *No,* none of it is happenstance or coincidental.

Of course, any earnest student of the Bible knows that Nehemiah contains at least two other essential features in its content: (1) It reports significant facts about Israel's post-Babylonian-captivity history; and (2) it contains a beautiful study in principles of leadership that can bring about the cooperation of believers and enable their effective work together. Those uses of Nehemiah are obvious, and I wasn't then, nor am I now, minimizing them. But this is possibly the most pronounced picture in the Bible of how God is ready to achieve one of the most challenging problems faced by His children.

> *Nehemiah is loaded with lessons in the Holy Spirit's ways
> of working to bring about the recovery of broken people;
> to introduce health to the fullness of the human being,
> including bringing full redemption to our personalities.*

I want to join you in pressing forward in God's Word—moving into a study of *third* purpose and application of the book of Nehemiah. It's for us, Sir! It is clearly intended and not accidental—something of God's New Testament intent for our use of this Old Testament portion of His Word.

Here is a guidebook on how the Holy Spirit is ready to come to assist us in rebuilding our brokenness, to strengthen our weaknesses and to lead us past our ignorance and into victory beyond our past habits of defeat.

Here is a forecast of what God is doing today in the lives of so many men who are realizing anew their need to rely on "the consoling breath or Spirit of God" as they recommit themselves to being God's men.

Here are principles that men can use in rebuilding their families— which, as we each confess are those points where we may have abandoned our responsibilities in pursuit of success, or violated our trust in pursuing the "feel good" mood of a culture that has led so many men away from home, wife and children.

We are more than people who need rebirth—we need rebuilding as well. And the Holy Spirit, whose workings are released in our lives when we receive Jesus Christ the Lord, awaits each of us who will join

Him in that holy partnership He offers—toward the rebuilding of every part of our lives that is less than a present praise to God.

In faith, let's begin to praise Him now! The hymn we quoted previously began with the promise of the Comforter's coming. The balance of it concludes our thoughts very well:

> The long, long night is past,
>   the morning breaks at last.
> And hushed the dreadful wail
>   and fury of the blast,
> As o'er the golden hills
>   the day advances fast!
> The Comforter has come!
>
> Lo, the great King of kings,
>   with healing in His wings,
> To ev'ry captive soul
>   a full deliv'rance brings;
> And thro' the vacant cells
>   the song of triumph rings;
> The Comforter has come![10]

SPIRITUAL WORKOUT

1. What is your present conception or evaluation of the role of the Holy Spirit in your life?
2. Are you aware of any limitations or preconditions you have placed on the Spirit's work?
3. Read John 14:17. What kind of person cannot receive the Spirit, and what does this description mean?
4. In what areas of your life, particularly as a man, do you sense the need for a divine Helper? Specify points you see as needful of "recovery" or "restoration."
5. Read Ephesians 6:10-20. Is the Christian's "armor" for earthly or spiritual battle? What part do you see the reference to the Spirit (v. 18) meaning or playing in our response and entry into "warfare"?

CHAPTER FOUR

GETTING LIFE BACK TOGETHER

The Word:

Nehemiah 1:3

And they said to me, "The survivors who are left from the captivity in the province are there in great distress and reproach. The wall of Jerusalem is also broken down, and its gates are burned with fire."

The Target:

- To distinguish the difference between the two features of our humanity that were lost when sin entered the race: (1) our relationship *with* God, and (2) our rulership *under* God.
- To show the parallel between Jerusalem's rebuilt Temple (and our reborn spirit, through salvation), and Jerusalem's ruined walls (and the yet-to-be-restored parts of our lives/living/personalities).
- To remove the sense of guilt that often accrues due to the length of time it takes for certain aspects of our spiritual lives to develop.
- To call forth a full partnership with the Holy Spirit, in order that we might have the assistance we need to fully rebuild those parts of our lives that have been damaged by our own failures, or by the things that have been done to us by others.

Getting Life Back Together

What happened when man 'fell'?" asked the Sunday School teacher. With a puzzled expression, the seven-year-old answered,

"I don't know (pause), did he bounce?"

Most people have a better idea than that of what is meant by the "fall of man," yet it is important to our study that we have an agreed viewpoint about this foundational event in human history.

The Fall summarizes in two words the fact that man was designed with a higher estate and an innately superior destiny than he now generally experiences or realizes. The entry of sin into the world drastically changed everything. Man, created perfectly "in the image of God,"[1] was designed for large purposes and deep fulfillment. His capacity for self-will (even for disobedience if he chose) was not an inherent flaw in his nature, but a necessary potential to his makeup if free will was to be available to him.

The opening chapters of Genesis set forth three essential truths:

1. Man was created in God's image and with unimaginably high destiny and purpose;
2. Man was given responsible dominion over the earth—a rule to be expressed in everything from family relationships to the mastery of the earth and cultivation of its resources through creative development;
3. Man's authority and ability to successfully exercise that rule would find its fountainhead in continued obedience to and worshipful relationship with his Creator.

Those three statements are worthy of a quick review, because the scope of their significance to you and me is more immediate than we might at first think. Looking at the originally created and divinely intended order, two things were clearly intended for mankind: *relationship* and *rulership*. Both are fundamental to our created purpose;

and both have been broken by the Fall. Without recovery, God's design for us and destiny through us is marred. We are unable to truly live without God, find fulfillment apart from Him or experience His purpose in us until the impact of the Fall is dealt with.

It is important that we each have a sense of man's purpose and the dimensions of loss in his fall, for unless we perceive something of what has been lost, we won't know what we might expect to be regained through the full salvation Christ has purchased.

BEYOND THE NEW BIRTH:
GOD'S REDEMPTIVE PURPOSE

For the most part, Christian preaching and teaching focus only on restoring people to a relationship with God; showing how the cross of Jesus Christ has bridged the chasm sin caused between God and man, and how salvation offers man a way back to God. Of course this message is absolutely necessary and is fundamental as a starting point of understanding. We must be born again![2]

But if we stop there, with the acknowledgment of our need for a restored relationship, we may fail to perceive God's full redemptive purpose for fallen man. The restored relationship is primary in sequence, but does not conclude God's purpose in life for us. His desire is our return to restored rulership.

What does "rulership" have to do with life? Well, to begin, it means a recovery of self-control, of personal identity, of stabilized temperament and character. It means to "rule" in the sense that a fulfillment of Romans 5:17 would suggest that "those who receive abundance of grace and of the gift of righteousness will reign in life through the One, Jesus Christ."

Let me tell you, by way of illustration, about Jake Whitworth (not his real name). Like Adam, Jake had once been in relationship with God. But in the oil fields of a distant state, far from friends who might raise their eyebrows at his behavior, Jake became rougher than a "roughneck" has to be. He frequented the bars, hurled his huge frame into countless fights and, at will, turned the air blue with profanity.

Then Jake met Jesus. This time, he *really* met the Lord. From the vantage point of his restored relationship with God, Jake was embarrassed about the way he had denied Him by his lifestyle. A lesser man may have moved away so he could start over without the stigma of his former life. But not Jake! You might be startled at what he did.

Having become established in Christ, Jake eventually went back into those bars! This time, however, it was with a new quality of life resonating; with a testimony on his lips instead of profane words; and an authority over sin in his life, instead of being ruled by booze, brawling and a bad mouth. By the power of the Holy Spirit filling his life, Jake began to rebuild the reputation he had lost with the character he had regained. In other words, he recovered the self-control, the personal identity, the stabilized temperament and character—the rulership—that God had originally purposed for him. God's grace by God's Spirit worked a restoration in him in the very environment where he had earlier violated the Creator's order for his life and purpose.

And it is this rulership, this "reigning now in life"—God's follow-through goal in His redemptive purpose—that is at the heart of our studying Nehemiah's assistance to the citizens dwelling amid the rubble that was Jerusalem. The essence of the project he led them in did not focus on their restored relationship with God—illustrated in their return and in the rebuilding of the Temple. Nehemiah's leadership of the people focused on what we well may call "a restored rulership"—the recovery of a godly people's identity as self-governing and upon their city's restored appearance as a capital center of righteousness.

The opening conversation between Nehemiah and Hanani, a relative who visited him with a report from the returned exiles in Jerusalem, reveals the crux of concern:

"How is it going with our brethren who have returned to Judah?" Nehemiah inquires.

"Those who have returned are in great distress and reproach," Hanani laments. Nehemiah probes further:

"What's the cause of their problem?"

"The wall of Jerusalem is broken down and its gates are burned."

With that brief explanation, Hanani's complaint focused on the embarrassment of a people who already had solid, historic evidence of a relationship with God. He had fulfilled His Word of promise, returning the Jewish families to their land, and He had blessed them as they pursued rebuilding the Temple—visiting them as they reestablished worship there. In other words, their relationship was restored and their worship was pure.

But notwithstanding the joy of that right relationship with God, the people recognized the incompleteness of their situation: "We have a Temple, but our capital city—our center of government—is a shambles."

You see, without a wall the city was open prey to oppressors. With destroyed gates there was no way of keeping back an adversary and no focus of government, for in ancient times the city gates were the seat of local rule. In short, they had a life with God but had no evidence of it affecting the practical details of day-to-day living.

Sound familiar? Perhaps not necessarily in your own life, but have you found this problem among dear believers who are indeed reborn, but whose lives are not at all rebuilt? Can you remember such a time in your own life? Or see anything like that now?

They were embarrassed. After all, Jerusalem was their representative city—their "face" to the world around. But even though their Temple had been rebuilt, the rest of the city and the walls surrounding it were nothing but rubble. How vulnerable they were to the mockery of their critics and enemies:

"Some God you worship in that Temple! Look at the mess you call your capital city. Apparently your God has little concern for or no ability in the practical issues of life! Your 'heaven-hoped-for' life looks to us like it's no earthly good!"

Have you ever sensed this dilemma yourself? Are you born again, yet parts of your personality are a contradiction to the power of the God you worship? Might someone justly point a finger and challenge, "Big deal! Some new birth. Look at the mess...!"?

I have no desire to register shame or condemnation: No! But the key to building with the Spirit is to gain discernment about where the rebuilding needs to take place. Begin now to open to Him, even as you read.

In the exercises at the end of this chapter you'll have opportunity to respond to some of these questions I've raised, along with others. After taking note of details in your life and knowing how true it is that so much is "broken down and burned with fire," you could feel that same sense of reproach and distress Hanani expressed to Nehemiah. But if there is any point in your life at which you feel vulnerable to any justified criticism of practical weaknesses in the structure of your life for Christ—Brother, *take hope!*

Nehemiah's message is about people who had a relationship with

God, but moved on in that relationship—*built with His assistance*— to recover their potential to function during life's challenges, problems and practical details. And *that's* what it means to "reign in life," as the Bible says, or as our contemporary lingo puts it, to "get it all together."

GOD DOESN'T EVEN HAVE TO ACTIVATE MOST INSTANCES OF JUDGMENT UPON SIN. THE VAST MAJORI-TY OF HUMAN SINNING CARRIES WITHIN ITSELF THE DEADLY SEEDS OF ITS OWN PENALTY.

So, we go deeper into Nehemiah—this handbook on our potential of recovering *in life's nitty-gritty* what's been broken or lost by the impact of sin's damage in our pasts. We see the hope that our restored relationships with God can be matched by a restoration of rulership:

a. By regained self-control and purpose, things that threaten a sense of personal security or confidence (gates); and
b. By a reconstruction of any shattered aspects of our self-understanding or identity (walls).

THE RUBBLE OF THE PAST

Look at Israel in its past sin. As a nation, they had walked in disobedience, and because they had failed God, judgment came upon them. And in discussing "judgment," I think it's important to understand the concept. Essentially, I would hope people would understand that such "judgments" are not so much direct acts of God's anger as much as they are simply the inevitable result of violating life's protocols—of disobedience to the laws God has given to help us avoid the devastation sin brings down upon our heads.

If we could see the heart of the heavenly Father, we would find that

God is injured and grieved when, through rebellion or ignorance, any of us pursue our own way unto our own destruction. Yet His judgment is never vindictive. In fact, for the most part, God doesn't even have to activate most instances of judgment upon sin. The vast majority of human sinning carries within itself the deadly seeds of its own penalty. When the sin is sown, the judgment is as sure as harvest. People introduce judgment upon their own heads and, as the Jerusalem of Nehemiah's time testified, the destruction distilling from even a preceding generation's failures often leaves a sad residue to be inherited by their offspring. And as wondrous as our salvation is, coming to the Savior does not immediately solve some of the long-term results of sin.

However, knowing Christ *does* bring us in touch with resources for dealing with sin's residue. The indwelling of His Holy Spirit brings a presence which, if we will draw upon His aid, can introduce a supernatural capability for recovery and rebuilding. As Joel's prophecy said (see his chapter 2), foretelling the coming work of the Holy Spirit, "What the caterpillar (and other insects destroying the crops) has taken, I will restore!"

And so it was that even though Israel had returned and built their Temple—and had even praised their God as a people—the rubble surrounding their Temple gave little evidence of a true "place." Jerusalem was a shambles, not a city. And how often does it depict what is true of the reborn? How often does the paradox appear: people who know God and are known of Him, but whose sense of "person" has been dispossessed by all that's gone before? Have you ever struggled with questions such as:

- Why can't I shut depressive thoughts out of my mind?
- Why am I so shaken by fears?
- What causes my inability to defend against temptation? I feel like it's threatening to overcome me.
- Why do feelings of worthlessness prevail?

Shouldn't our restored relationship with God be enough to keep out unwanted thoughts and demeaning attitudes? Or is there another aspect of our salvation available and waiting to be appropriated? Can the Lord reinstate His rule in me just as He has reinstated my relationship with Him?

The answer: *Absolutely!*

And the starting place is to see both (a) the need and goal of such recovery, and (b) the fact that it takes time for our recovery.

PATIENCE WITH PROGRESS

Many believers have such a struggle trying to learn to walk as steadfast disciples of Christ while still so very crippled from their pasts. Although in sincerity they seek to speed ahead, before long they become frustrated and confused, especially when they see others who are progressing steadily.

But to become a new creature in Christ is only the beginning of this new life. The promise, "If any man be in Christ, he is a new creature,"[3] does not instantly guarantee completed products. It does promise a new world of possibility opening to us; we are no longer dominated or controlled by our pasts. But for the full dominion of Christ's rule to penetrate the whole personality, in most cases "the real you" needs to be rebuilt by the Spirit.

Consider the radically different testimony of two "reborn babes" who came to Christ in my own congregation.

Thelma stepped into my office one Saturday afternoon in tears, having just been kicked out of their apartment by her husband. He was a satanist and they had both been heavily involved in the occult before her conversion to Christ. Her past involved a great deal of rejection by her parents and personal violation by her father. Though she was highly intelligent, and a product of one of America's finest universities, Thelma was virtually incoherent as she stood before me in tears. Here she was, bereft of support and the mother of two lovable little children who themselves were terribly confused by what was happening with Momma and Daddy.

This combination of factors shaping her present was a staggering load for a young Christian. Unquestionably, Thelma belonged to Christ—she was born again, and knew she was "saved." But the remnants of her past now converged to reduce her to an emotional basket case, a domestic wreck and a desperate spiritual dependent. Though she was a new creature in Christ, Thelma was a highly vulnerable babe who could hardly walk and was completely ignorant of what to do and how to do it. Jerusalem's description of "broken walls and burned gates" aptly fit her.

For the following five years I watched her grow through the Word, through a fellowship with the body of the congregation and with the assistance of good counselors on our pastoral staff. The rebuilding process was long, but she eventually became an adequate, recovered person. Having long since been forsaken by her husband, God later provided a godly young man as His gift, completing the redemption of her domestic past.⁴ I was witness to that marriage, and delight to tell you that in every way Thelma is restored and her children are lovely, stable, happy kids. She has become the name "Thelma"—an expression of "the will of God."

Edward is another story. He was the kind of convert pastors wish could happen every time. It was a joy watching him respond as he went from new birth to stable discipleship within several weeks of his conversion. Within months Ed was given some introductory leadership roles, and within three years moved into eldership. He has become fully recognized within the body of our church as a growing-to-strength servant of Jesus Christ.

When we look at the difference in the time of each one's growth, we might be tempted to see Edward's responses as more mature than Thelma's. But we are wiser if we understand how different were his former "walls" from hers: the degree of devastation to the personality was in no way comparable.

Edward's family background was solid and secure, having parents who lovingly raised him. He never knew the pain of parental rejection, and most of his life was spent experiencing every cultural, financial, educational, intellectual and emotional benefit a young man can receive. Moreover, he was raised in the context of a Christianized environment, in a church that reverenced God. Even though the Word of God, as well as all of our need for new life in Christ, was *not* taught there, the social influence was redemptive and moral values honored. So, even though Ed had never heard the message of salvation, he did have some knowledge of the Bible (as information) and had been raised with a genuine desire for spiritual reality. Further, when he came to the Lord, he was already successful in business, fully emotionally stable, plus economically and professionally secure. The simple fact is that Edward had little from which to recover.

Sure, Ed needed Jesus! He needed spiritual rebirth—everyone does. And he accepted the responsibility of a new believer to open to real discipleship in the Lord, just as we all should. But the difference in the speed with which Edward and Thelma became established was drastically different, even though today their relative strength in Christ is virtually equal.

The point of their stories is to dramatize the fact that some of us who have been Christians for years still have Thelmalike problems hanging on from our pasts. Perhaps they are not as drastic in their implications as Thelma's were, but they still cause a lot of struggling.

Sadly, some precious "Thelmas" compare themselves with the "Edwards" of their congregations, and feel guilty. They wish they knew how to get from where they are to where they want to be as Jesus' dis-

---

THE "GRIT AND DETERMINATION" PROGRAM...IS NOTH-
ING MORE THAN A PROGRAM OF WORKS BUILT ON
GRACE, AND GIVEN TIME, THE TEMPORARY WALLS OF
SELF-WORKED RIGHTEOUSNESS WILL CRUMBLE.

---

ciples. And they become discouraged, all of us being so slow to find the truth that sheer grit and determination, as honorable as they are while they last, aren't the answer. Without the Holy Spirit's mightiness and partnership in the "rebuilding" process, weariness will usually take over.

The "grit and determination" program depends upon the relative degree of the individual's own strength, and as admirable as the temporary fruit may be, it isn't God's better way. Such discipleship will either end in discouragement or in self-righteousness; either in giving up because "I don't have what it takes," or in an inner smugness, based on the seeming success of my personal zeal. This isn't "discipleship": it is nothing more than a program of works built on grace, and given time, the temporary walls of self-worked righteousness will crumble.

Where do you sense you "fit" on the spectrum of "Edward" at one end and "Thelma" at the other? Whatever the case, I will only experience the fullest sense of Christ's Kingdom rule in all my life as I allow the Holy Spirit to work His "wholeness" in all of my personality. On any terms, that will take time. Some issues may be changed overnight, simply through instant obedience to God's Word and its principles. But other problems of personal difficulty—character weaknesses due to former habit or family traits, or moral, emotional or spiritual residue still present from the impact of my past sinning—all these require time.

It's a law of spiritual life and development: In some parts of our lives only "rebuilding" will accomplish what is needed to make our lives "work." Only "rebirth" in Christ can bring about the *atmosphere* that will make possible our complete wholeness, and that happens immediately when we're saved. But within that "atmosphere" of the newborn soul, there are *achievements* that only the Holy Spirit's help can bring about—often, needing His redeveloping grace in our lives for years.

The need for a *rebuilding stage* is normal in our lives as believers in Jesus. The pathway of progress is clear, also: (1) Identify your "broken walls and burned gates." (2) Partner with "Nehemiah." (3) Get down to specifics in this partnership by using the "Spiritual Workout" exercises. And in it all, (4) Ask "the consoling Spirit of God" (remember the meaning of Nehemiah's name?) to be your constant companion and enabler in the process of rebuilding.

To Summarize...

Looking into Nehemiah, this striking, historic picture of those broken, burned walls—so emblematic of our own personalities—reminds us: Not all the challenges I deal with are a direct result of my own sin. Indeed, I've contributed my share to my problems! But it helps keep our perspective at times to remember: Many new believers are still inheritors of personal and situational conditions that may not have actually been due to their own actions. Just as Jerusalem's destruction (and now, the broken walls inherited) was the price of a previous generation's failure, so it is with us at times.

These observations are no attempt to whitewash the fact that we have all contributed to a large share of our problems. But it is appropriate to note that all the answers to our own struggles are not instantly provided through rebirth. Nor is rebuilding always instantly realized—however sincere our dedication or rigid our efforts at self-disciplines.

It isn't a concession to self-pity or to doubt to identify such "residue from the past." It's a realistic step toward learning to "reign in life" through the Holy Spirit's help. Be realistic about:

- Inherited difficulties or personality weaknesses "transmitted" to you from an earlier generation;
- "Transmissions" through misunderstanding or mistreatment, ministered by parents or other authority figures, however unwittingly or intentionally it all may have been;
- How often such events stamp individuals with lifelong scars—unless recovery occurs (Childhood innocence is often tainted by adult ignorance and without redemptive action, permanent emotional disability may be experienced. We have only to think of the tragic case of "crack babies," who suffer through no fault of their own from their own mother's addiction to crack cocaine.);
- Transmissions of "genetic" inclinations, remembering that "genetics" are not only biological, but that spiritual, emotional and mental influences are too seldom discerned.

Why all this "self-searching"? Well, it isn't to psychoanalyze ourselves and thereby rationalize the reasons for our weaknesses or recurrent problems! Instead, we're looking at these points of "residue" because we have been offered a "Restorer"—the Nehemiah of the New Testament—the Holy Spirit! He has come to set in motion His program of full recovery for every part of our beings and our personalities.

He has come to partner with us in building until we look and operate like "the city of the great King"—until our souls become a worthy "capital city" under the government of Christ, as He exercises rule with fruitfulness and effectiveness in every detail of our lives.

So where do we begin?

SPIRITUAL WORKOUT

1. Review the story of Jake Whitworth, and decide what it speaks to you of truth and hope.
2. Can you identify specific places where your "walls"—your personality—has been eroded, broken, weakened or

severely damaged through scarring experiences or through sinful failure?

3. To deal with this, define your sense of how to be open to receiving the Holy Spirit as your helper; toward partnering with His enabling assistance at recovery from those points of pain or weakness.

4. Have you ever felt that you were experiencing the certain consequences of disobedience? Have you been tempted to feel guilt again, rather than to know these are signals to draw on fresh grace for full restoration?

5. Do you feel you lack patience—toward yourself or toward others—in the slow process of progress in rebuilding the walls of your life, your character, your personality?

6. What are some ways you sense you may have inherited certain points of struggle—i.e., been "genetically impacted," either socially, spiritually, mentally or emotionally?

CHAPTER FIVE

RECOGNIZING YOUR MAKEUP

The Word:

Nehemiah 1:3,4

And they said to me, "The survivors who are left from the captivity in the province are there in great distress and reproach. The wall of Jerusalem is also broken down, and its gates are burned with fire." So it was, when I heard these words, that I sat down and wept, and mourned for many days; I was fasting and praying before the God of heaven.

The Target:

- To explain the structure of the human personality—spirit, soul and body—and to show the Bible's clarity of distinction between soul and spirit.
- To show why it is important to understand the function of each part of the "soul," since the interplay of intellect, emotion and will determines everything about our lives.
- To show the parallel between the "soul" and the "walls" of Jerusalem; not merely as an interesting analogy, but as a dramatic picture to help us relate to the Holy Spirit's will to help us unto restoration.
- To point to the areas of self-inquiry we might make, which may help us more readily respond to and participate with the Holy Spirit as He comes to help us at specific points of need for "rebuilding" in our lives.

RECOGNIZING YOUR MAKEUP

Anna loves jigsaw puzzles. I've lived with her for more than three and a half decades, and I am always amazed at her patience and persistence with those piles of tiny cardboard pieces that finally end up depicting so beautiful a scene. She doesn't work on very many, but almost every Christmas season she'll pour a box of bits on the table and invite everyone to join her.

I'm usually the most reluctant participant. My limited involvement never hinders the accomplishing of her project though, because kids or grandkids are always present and friends or other relatives visit, who— just as my wife—*love* jigsaw puzzles.

You may be as enthusiastic about them as Anna, or as slow to action on one as I am, but we've all dabbled with jigsaw puzzles enough to experience the irritation of discovering missing pieces. Surely that's happened to you. You find yourself looking under the table, behind the cushions, beneath the couch, chairs and other furniture, wondering where those supposedly lifeless objects have wandered. At times you'd swear they had legs! But the search goes on, and for one obvious reason: *You want to see the WHOLE picture!*

Not dissimilar to the frustration felt when the entire scene escapes the worker of a puzzle, I've seen the frustration of people who wish they had "the whole picture" of God's purpose in their lives. So often, the picture of God's purpose eludes them because of another "puzzle" that eludes too many good people: the "pieces" of the human personality are not so much missing as not fitting together as intended. For example, a fundamental point of bewilderment begins with not knowing the difference between "soul" and "spirit."

That distinction, just as a beginning point, is far more than an academic issue. Can you really imagine the people of Nehemiah's day supposing that the completed, rebuilt Temple rendered the need for rebuilding of the city walls unnecessary? They may have been hindered from their recovering those walls, and embarrassed because of it, but they knew the difference. And yet, how many believers think of the soul and spirit as synonyms, rather than recognizing the difference in "those pieces of the puzzle." The truth is that just as clearly different as Jerusalem's broken walls were from her rebuilt Temple, so different is the yet-being-rebuilt-soul of the believer in contrast with his/her renewed/reborn spirit.

One of the reasons many of us have difficulty responding to the Holy Spirit's efforts to lead us into a full rebuilding of our lives, characters, habits and conduct is that we don't have a picture of what He's trying to do. So let's take some time and look into the importance of knowing the distinction between the soul and spirit. Since the Holy Spirit wants to rebuild all brokenness of soul, it will help to know exactly what goes on there.

DISCERNING BETWEEN SPIRIT, SOUL AND BODY

The Bible makes a clear distinction between the human spirit, soul and body. The difference between our physical bodies and the other two, of course, is not difficult to compute. But the difference between soul and spirit, and the way that each relates to the other, including our bodies, is important to learn—just in terms of self-understanding.

Let's begin with the revelation of God's Word, and the way the Holy Spirit has shown us that these parts of us are each unique from the other.

Contrary to some opinion, soul and spirit are not one and the same: In Luke 1:46,47 after Elizabeth has greeted her and confirmed her having conceived the Messiah, Mary sang, *"My soul magnifies the Lord, and my spirit has rejoiced in God my Savior."*

The difference is important enough to know that God's Word functions to give this discernment: Hebrews 4:12 states: *"For the word of God is living and powerful, and sharper than any two-edged sword, piercing even to the division of soul and spirit, and of joints and marrow, and is a discerner of the thoughts and intents of the heart."*

There is a fundamental wholeness that is desirable and available for each part of our being: In 1 Thessalonians 5:23 Paul prayed for the Thessalonians: *"Now may the God of peace Himself sanctify you completely; and may your whole spirit, soul, and body be preserved blameless at the coming of our Lord Jesus Christ."*[1]

It is clearly significant to notice that the Bible not only makes a clean distinction between the spirit and soul, but also goes further. The Word declares that one of the functions of the Scriptures is to discern between the two.[2] That is to say, soul and spirit are not only shown as distinct, but avoiding confusion as to which is which in our personalities—and how we respond to each—is important enough that we are called to learn to *discern* between them.

God's Word doesn't present the fact that we have three parts to our being for reasons of philosophical argument. Neither is the tripartite nature of persons some hangover of ancient thought to be replaced today by newer notions. No, God reveals the structure of our being by His Word, and because He wants to accomplish distinct things in each part of us, He wants us to understand about each part—from His Word.

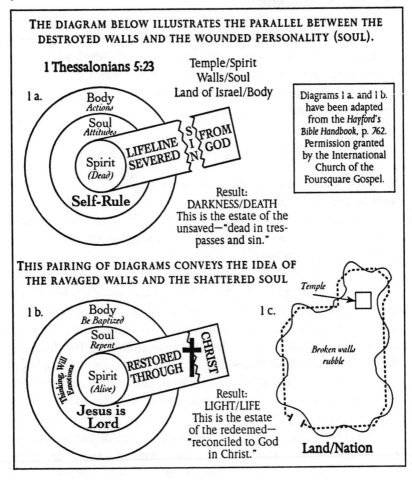

THE DIAGRAM BELOW ILLUSTRATES THE PARALLEL BETWEEN THE DESTROYED WALLS AND THE WOUNDED PERSONALITY (SOUL).

1 Thessalonians 5:23

Temple/Spirit
Walls/Soul
Land of Israel/Body

1 a.
Body *Actions*
Soul *Attitudes*
Spirit *(Dead)*
LIFELINE SEVERED SIN FROM GOD
Self-Rule

Diagrams 1 a. and 1 b. have been adapted from the *Hayford's Bible Handbook*, p. 762. Permission granted by the International Church of the Foursquare Gospel.

Result:
DARKNESS/DEATH
This is the estate of the unsaved—"dead in trespasses and sin."

THIS PAIRING OF DIAGRAMS CONVEYS THE IDEA OF THE RAVAGED WALLS AND THE SHATTERED SOUL

1 b.
Body *Be Baptized*
Soul *Repent*
Thinking, Will, Emotions
Spirit *(Alive)*
RESTORED THROUGH CHRIST
Jesus is Lord

Result:
LIGHT/LIFE
This is the estate of the redeemed—"reconciled to God in Christ."

1 c.
Temple
Broken walls rubble
Land/Nation

The geographic setting in the text of our Nehemiah study provides an interesting and helpful parallel to the structure of our own beings.

First, consider the Temple: Central to the city and central to worship, it can be likened to the inner man—*the human spirit.* Sin destroys our relationship with God and our capacity to worship Him. Rebirth in Christ—just as a reconstructed Temple—makes renewed worship and fellowship with God a living possibility "in **spirit** and truth."[3]

Second, consider the city: Central to the rule of the surrounding land or territory, it can be likened to the center of individual choice—*the human soul.* Just as the walls and gates had been ruined by sin's judgment, so the impact of sin in the personality deteriorates the human capacity to will to live under God's will and rule—to "reign in life" through Jesus Christ.

Third, consider the environs: This area is intended to be a land of peace and fruitful harvest and can be likened to *the human body.* Through it, God may channel and manifest His Kingdom witness; or, on the other hand, we may allow the body to manifest actions (to "manifest a harvest," so to speak) that contradict or violate the Living God who is worshiped at the center of our being.

THE FOCUS IS ON THE SOUL

Nehemiah's dismay was specifically directed toward the fact that the walls of the city remained broken down long after the Temple was restored. The previously mentioned parallel holds true here. The focus of concern on the walls parallels our need to see the Holy Spirit's desire to "restore my soul."

This is what Paul is talking to the Ephesians about when he says, *"Put off...the old man which grows corrupt according to the deceitful lusts, and be renewed in the spirit of your mind"* (Eph. 4:22,23). The words "be renewed in *the spirit of your mind"* indicate how the intellect/thoughts (mind) needed to be controlled by the "new" in their lives—the Holy Spirit residing within, rather than by the spirit of the world around them. (This is why, several verses later, Paul contrasts the potential of being either manipulated by the devil [see 4:27] or being continually refilled with the Holy Spirit [see 5:18].)

To read the whole passage is to see that a group of people who are well established in salvation's grace (see chapters 1 and 2) are being addressed about our very human struggles with everything from the crude and the lewd (see 4:17-24) to reckless words, anger, lying and unforgiveness (see 4:25-32). Simply put, their "Temple" (spirit) was reborn, but their "Walls" (soul) still needed rebuilding. This helps us understand his plea to reborn believers, calling on them *not* to be unresponsive to the Holy Spirit (see 4:30), but to allow Him to enable them to grow—be built up—in the will of God (see 5:17,18).

To see these things from the standpoint of "soul and spirit," we are assisted in seeing that those early believers were no different from us. When they are called to leave their former patterns of living behind, the writer is not addressing willful scoundrels. In this Epistle as in

―――

THE HUMAN *WILL* IS THE MOST AWESOME FEATURE OF THE SOUL—INDEED, OF YOUR WHOLE BEING—FOR IT DETERMINES DESTINY.

―――

most of the New Testament, they—as we—are addressed as "saints" (spiritually alive in Christ); but struggles in the *soul,* unless discerned and defended through recovered "walls," expose the "saint" to being dominated by past failures and world-spirited practices.

Here in our study text is an Old Testament picture of this New Testament truth. Hear it in Nehemiah's words: "So it was, when I heard these words [Hanani's report], that I sat down and wept."[4] We can hear the echo of the Holy Spirit's "grief"—His present concern about the activities of some reborn yet still "broken" souls. It is precisely what is expressed in the same Epistle referenced above, as Paul appeals to these believers in Ephesians 4:30: *"And do not grieve the Holy Spirit of God, by whom you were sealed for the day of redemption"* (i.e., trade-marked as belonging to God Almighty—"sealed" *in* your spirit, *by* His Spirit [see Eph. 1:13]).

What a striking, overwhelmingly moving parallel!

Even though the spirit had been reborn (restored Temple), the apostle Paul calls to them to no longer walk (a) with a "darkened understanding"—with a worldly mind, or (b) as those who live "past feeling"—led by worldly emotions.[5] He is dealing with "soulish" behavior, because the "understanding" (intellect) and "feelings" (emotion) are operational there, in the soul.

This whole matter explodes into light in the understanding when we look closely at the way the human soul works—that is, what its component parts are and how they interact.

The soul includes three essential facets and functions that essentially comprise the personality:

1. The intellect—the processes of our intelligence, our minds, our thoughts, our reasoning powers;
2. The emotions—the processes of our temperaments, our feelings, our attitudes, our moods; and
3. The will—the processes of our choices, our decisions, our determination or our willfulness.

Most of what lures, drives, attracts, convinces, persuades or motivates you is generated at the thought (intellect) or feeling (emotions) level. Affected by this interplay of intellect and emotion is your will, the decision-making center of your soul.

The human *will* is the most awesome feature of the soul—indeed, of your whole being—for it determines destiny. By reason of the will, the soul functions as the command center of the whole personality. (Hereby we understand the ultimate issue in the words, "The soul who sins shall die."[6])

What goes on in my soul determines how I feel and what attitude will motivate me today (my emotions). What goes on in my soul decides how I think, and what I will learn today (my intellect).

But beyond the "input" of my emotions and intellect, what goes on in my soul will decide what actions or choices I will make today (my will):

• Those lessons I must know to grow in the understanding of the Lord.
• Those feelings I need to respond to or reject to obey the will of God.
• Those attitudes or facts I need to process according to the Holy Spirit's directives.

All of this is occurring in my soul—day to day. And how my mind and emotions interactionally function will generate decisions that either deepen my problems or release my progress.

With this understanding, the absolute need for my soul to be restored—to be *built by the Spirit*—becomes clearer than ever. My reborn spirit may make possible the reality and sincerity of my worship to God, but it will be by the rebuilding of my soul that I determine the quality and character of my service for Him.

That Nehemiah's tears and the Holy Spirit's grief both center on the unfinished residue of brokenness (the walls and gates, which compare with the soul—intellect and emotions) calls us to focus on that part of our being where the rebuilding process is most needed. It is more than coincidental that it was the *walls* that caused Nehemiah's tears and it is our *souls* that can cause the Holy Spirit to grieve.

Gaining this introductory insight, we can begin to see and understand ourselves as God's Word describes our humanity: spirit, soul and body. When our spirits are reborn, our bodies are subject to our direction (in contrast to our being manipulated like puppets by the world-spirit prior to our salvation'). Now, our souls function like a "middle-man"—determining what of our new lives will be translated into new living. The will—the command center of the soul—sits in the driver's seat. If it is in any way dysfunctional or disobedient—by reason of unrecovered weakness due to past habit, a residue of pain, or unrepaired brokenness—the whole person is affected:

- Unworthy feelings, unhealed emotions or embittered attitudes may dictate the will's surrender to temper tantrums, lust or otherwise;
- Unbiblical reasonings, doubts or impure thoughts may shade the intellect and taint the mind's "input" to my choices and actions.

Just as broken walls hindered the definition and control of the city, so the saved but unrestored human soul can hinder the real progress of God's intended purpose in me as His redeemed child.

As the seat of the identity and will, the soul functions as the command center of the human being. What goes on there determines the extent to which the King's rule—i.e., the reign of the kingdom of

God—will be manifest in the whole of my being. If brokenness or malfunction exists there, it may not mean my eternal damnation, for my spirit has been "sealed unto the day of redemption." But what a shame if my soul's responses to life cause great dismay to the precious Holy Spirit, and at the same time occasion great embarrassment to myself or others who know I belong to Christ. None of us want to continue as a contradiction on the outside of the miracle God has worked on us *inside*.

All of us want the Lord to be glorified in all our thoughts and all our feelings, so that all our choices advance us in His way and in His will. Thus the reconditioning of our souls becomes a project of highest priority.

ACTION AHEAD

In Nehemiah's concerned tears we can see a prophetic picture of the Holy Spirit's compassionate grief over any need or weakness we have, and the fruit of this concern is that He will act. Just as Nehemiah was moved to action, in the same way we can count on the Holy Spirit. He is moved with an understanding of our need and He is ready to bring aid to the site of any weakness in our souls.

His action will address specific areas of brokenness.

All of us share so much in common when it comes to need for being "built by the Spirit." Emotionally, how many of us carry scars or emotional residue from childhood experiences, from recent sin, suffering or tragic instances of disappointment? Some events leave scars on the *psyche* (the Greek word for "soul"). Often such scars remain even when the scarring event itself seems to have long since been forgotten.

Then, add to emotionally caused "wounds of the soul," those which are registered at the mental or intellectual level—in the mind. A habit here, an insensitiveness there, a loss of capacity to respond—these are issues of "broken walls," and they determine so much of how life is lived as we respond from brokenness or wholeness.

Often what happened to you in early years breeds insecurity. Like a broken wall, no established boundary of identity or secured line of defense exists. In the same way "broken walls" hinder the capacity of the mind to resist unwanted ideas and cripple strength of emotion to be courageous or stable in crises.

Question: Why don't I seem to be able to resist temptation?

Answer: Could the basic reason be that crumbled walls and burned gates—burned with the hellfire of a past lifestyle—have now left you with no adequate "line of defense"?

Question: Why am I so easily overcome by doubt or by habit?

Answer: Could it be that the personality is spongy because the solidity of fixed walls is absent due to the mind's exposure—past or present—to ideas or thought patterns that cripple the capacity for resistance?

Beyond this, think of how much plain physical sickness may be related to the soul's broken walls. Physicians and psychologists attest that physical sickness is often the direct result of mental or emotional upheaval. Our souls (psyche) impact our bodies (soma) and our physical afflictions are often psychosomatic—signs of deeper pain within our personality.

How crucial a center is our soul!

How needful its rebuilding unto wholeness!

WHAT ABOUT YOU?

Are some things going on in your mind that hinder your spiritual growth? Do you feel like those people in the book of Nehemiah—a reproach and an embarrassment to yourself so that you feel weakened or crippled in the face of your enemies?

- At the mental level, do doubts become a real difficulty?
- How often does your imagination hinder you to the point that it interferes with where you really want to go?
- What about impure thoughts?
- What about the inability to focus?
- Do your thoughts digress to the unimportant and insignificant?
- How many times do your reasoning capabilities argue against you rather than work for you?

- How many times do things going on in your mind torment you and make you feel incapable of withstanding them?

I'm not talking about a lack in intellect; the issue has nothing to do with your IQ. I'm addressing the rubble—the things that don't seem to cooperate with what God is wanting to do, and the part of you that cries out to have "the mind of Christ."

And what about the "emotional you"?

- Do fears surround you?
- Do lusts clamor for attention, eroding your inner integrity and trying to prompt decisions to feed them?
- Does anger fester, embittering your attitude toward others?
- Has unforgiveness lodged deep within, hindering the kind of spiritual growth you'd like to have?

Oh, how these mental and emotional forces work against our will! They cripple our confidence, hinder our attempts to move ahead and weaken our resistance. And it all has to do with a soul needing restoration at points of loss.

Yet, amid all this and deeper still, dear friend, remember there is an inner core of God—established hope—your redeemed spirit! Let that love, peace and joy abide and secure your heart:

- He has secured the Temple within!
- Your reborn spirit is alive toward Him!
- That life within guarantees the presence of the Holy Spirit!

NEHEMIAH! THE HOLY SPIRIT
IS PRESENT TO HELP!

Your spirit (the new you deep inside) loves God unashamedly and unabashedly, and you are owned—totally possessed by Him. You are saved and you know it. You have that deep, settled confidence—*I am the Lord's.* In the past you might have looked at yourself and wondered, *If I am the Lord's, why am I like this?* But the answer is now coming into view.

You are learning how God's restoration program is included in His gift of redemption in Christ. He regenerated you; He will restore you. God's plan of redemption for you includes a reborn spirit *and* a restored soul! He not only has brought you an *instant salvation in Christ*, making you **heaven-ready**; but He has sent His Holy Spirit to develop an *ongoing restoration increasingly*—a certainty that the recovery of all that has been stolen or broken in the past is going to be restored or rebuilt, and make you **earth-ready**: ready to live here and now, as well as forever with Him!

So, let's summarize. Your soul is constituted of:

    a. Your intellect—how you think;
    b. Your emotions—how you feel; and
    c. Your will—the choices you make.

All three are addressed in Paul's prayer: "May your whole spirit, soul and body be preserved blameless at the coming of our Lord Jesus Christ."[8] The Holy Spirit is still answering that prayer today. So freely and boldly join your prayer to that one: "Oh, God, according to Your promise, I welcome Your Holy Spirit to teach, to strengthen, to console and to restore me. Work Your wholeness in my whole personality and make me like Jesus!" Amen!

And what will the answer look like?

A father came into the den to discover his five-year-old had put a jigsaw puzzle with a map of the world together with amazing speed. Impressed, he asked,

"Joey, how did you get the map put together so fast?"

"Because, Daddy, on the other side was the picture of a man; and when I put the man together, it put the whole world together."

I predict "the picture" coming together for you, dear friend. When we begin to see how the pieces of our personality fit, and how the Holy Spirit has come to help us rebuild—our "whole world" comes together.

SPIRITUAL WORKOUT

    1. Just as most people have a dominant right or left hand, so spirit, soul or body may tend to dominate in some person-

alities. What part of you would you say tends to most influence your choices—mind or emotions? What do you think others of your family would say about your answer?

2. Narrowing your focus to the soul, which of its dimensions—the intellect, the emotions or the will—do you think is dominant in your personality?

3. What are some advantages and disadvantages of a man's having an underdeveloped emotional capacity?

4. Take time to draw your own diagram of the human makeup. Rehearse with a study partner the traits of each part and how they interplay upon one another.

5. What part of your being do you perceive as most needing the Holy Spirit's assistance in rebuilding?

6. Do a review of the book of Ephesians this week, noticing the relationship of the whole of this study to the balance that book gives to (a) our lives in Christ (secured), and (b) our lives in this world (under fire).

CHAPTER SIX

PRAYER THAT REBUILDS PEOPLE

The Word:

Nehemiah 1:4-11

So it was, when I heard these words, that I sat down and wept, and mourned for many days; I was fasting and praying before the God of heaven. And I said: "I pray, Lord God of heaven, O great and awesome God, You who keep Your covenant and mercy with those who love You and observe Your commandments, please let Your ear be attentive and Your eyes open, that You may hear the prayer of Your servant which I pray before You now, day and night, for the children of Israel Your servants, and confess the sins of the children of Israel which we have sinned against You. Both my father's house and I have sinned.

We have acted very corruptly against You, and have not kept the commandments, the statutes, nor the ordinances which You commanded Your servant Moses.

Remember, I pray, the word that You commanded Your servant Moses, saying, "If you are unfaithful, I will scatter you among the nations; but if you return to Me, and keep My commandments and do them, though some of you were cast out to the farthest part of the heavens, yet I will gather them from there, and bring them to the place which I have chosen as a dwelling for My name."

Now these are Your servants and Your people, whom You have redeemed by Your great power, and by Your strong hand. O Lord, I pray, please let Your ear be attentive to the prayer of Your servant, and to the prayer of Your servants who desire to fear Your name; and let Your servant prosper this day, I pray, and grant him mercy in the sight of this man." For I was the king's cupbearer.

The Target:

- To focus the importance of prayer as essential to the process of building or rebuilding a life according to God's promise and purpose.

- To examine the first prayer of the 17 in the book of Nehemiah, to see the pattern it discloses and the principles it reveals.

- To create a simple, childlike readiness to pray, in the confidence that Almighty God is ready to hear—and to answer.

- To point toward a dependence upon the Holy Spirit's assistance in prayer, and to the place obedience holds in opening the way to breakthrough in answers to prayer.

Prayer That Rebuilds People

Josh Billings, the wry old American humorist of another generation, used to say, "Never work before you eat your breakfast. But if you ever *have* to work before you eat your breakfast, *eat your breakfast first!*"

Let me rephrase Josh's counsel. Taking a look at our call by the Spirit to partner with Him in being built and rebuilt, "Never undertake any Spirit-directed project before you pray; but if the project demands action before you pray—*pray first.*"

Is prayer a special problem for men? Yeah! It really is!!

Is it our culture's emphasis on the pragmatic? Is it the difficulty of getting our own souls "on-line" with God—so easily distracted by the pressure of time, or disjointed in attempted focus by the tidal flow of our minds? I don't know about you, but I don't often find it easy to get focused, even when I've set time aside for prayer. Like waves sweeping up on the beach, splashes of thought and a certain degree of power occur, but often when I've found a moment of "touching Him," it seems the wave suddenly receded—and the tide went out.

If there's ever a case of seeing the practical results of a man's actions being borne along to success by the power of prayer, Nehemiah's prayer pattern, along with his work with the Jerusalem crowd, lays it out. From start to finish Nehemiah believed in, exercised the practice of and functioned in the power of prayer.

No less than 17 prayers are recorded in the 13 chapters of Nehemiah. To look at the first one is to see some basic truths that can help us understand the possibilities awaiting us through prayer and help us recognize where prayer's real power base is.

As we read and examine the text above, we'll find that Nehemiah's prayer actually sets the exact *tone, truth and thrust* of the kind of praying the Holy Spirit is ready to assist us in making. Our starting point is in committing to pray. Our will to pray is often weakened more by our human uncertainty than just our fleshly procrastination. Some very basic questions nag more of us than maybe would admit it:

- What can I pray for or about? (What are the legitimate boundaries, if any? I don't want to be airheaded or super-stitious.)
- When should I pray? (What are the rules? I mean, what if "early in the morning" doesn't work very well?)
- How can I pray *in* God's will (I don't want to be presump-tuous!)?
- How can I be sure I'm not praying selfishly?

...And (probably the worst question of all),

- Isn't it possible—just maybe!—that things will work out anyway? (Or, after they have "worked out," to hear your mind wondering—*How do I know my prayer had anything to do with it?*)

These uncertainties all have a way of breeding doubt or passivity toward prayer. But I think most of them can be resolved by settling just one thing...

PRAYER ISN'T "EARNING POINTS"

Before we actually analyze the principles demonstrated in Nehemiah's prayer, let me relieve you of one misconception: Contrary to many people's ideas, prayer is not another kind of "works" program; not a "build up credit on the heaven-side of things" plan. Oh yes, there is a ministry of prayer, and I'm not minimizing diligence in attending to it. But no program of prayer is a means by which you earn points with God, nor is praying a fleshly attempt to gain God's attention or favor through our human effort.

Jesus took some solid shots at humanistic notions about prayer that supposed saying the right words or striking the right pose will improve your chances with God (see Matt. 6:5-8). As a man seeking to grow in God's ways—and knowing prayer is fundamental to a walk with Him, I need to find a place of peace on some basics:

- Getting God to restore His image in you is not a reward He gives in response to a certain quantity of prayer.
- God is not looking down condescendingly, watching to see

when you have bowed and scraped enough to receive a holy fortune cookie, an ego-stroking pat on the head or a paternal smile.

Now, prayer is not a "works" program—a legislated system of acquiring merit and, thereby, results. But prayer *does* enter strongly into the

————

TIME IN GOD'S PRESENCE HAS NEVER BEEN MEANT TO BE AN *EARNING* TIME. INSTEAD, IT'S A *LEARNING* TIME.

————

development of my relationship with God, and it isn't because He gets to like me more, but because I get to know Him better. It has to do with *knowing* the Lord, with *understanding* His heart and ways, and with *gaining* His wisdom for facing and dealing with what I do.

- In prayer I'll come to learn more about God's person—His character.
- At prayer I'll discover how His nature starts to infuse mine with the qualities of His personality.
- Through prayer I'll experience restoration—there's healing in His presence.
- When praying, I'll have time to search my heart, my motives and my thoughts—in His presence; bringing discernment, confession, deliverance and insight for movement forward.

I'll learn about God before His Throne. And it's in that very setting, I'm most likely to learn about me...while I'm with *Him*.

So the "work at prayer and earn something good" idea has its back broken. Clearly, time in God's presence has never been meant to be an *earning* time. Instead, it's a *learning* time.

And with those thoughts as a preamble, join me as we read

Nehemiah's lead-off prayer in chapter 1:4-11. It's a tremendous model of its kind, where we can not only pick up on practical pointers but we can also derive tremendous hope. Brother, this is a prayer that result- ed in a restored city! If we can tune in to the principles here, there's reason to expect the same effective "building with the Spirit" to take place with us and those with whom we're in touch. Let's study this passage with a willingness and an expectancy: willing to welcome instruction from God's Word; expecting He wants to and will activate that Word in our living...and praying.

The record of Nehemiah's prayer shows some basic pointers to the pathway of prayer.

BEGIN WITH WORSHIP

> *So it was, when I heard these words, that I sat down and wept, and mourned for many days; I was fasting and pray- ing before the God of heaven. And I said: "I pray, Lord God of heaven, O great and awesome God, You who keep Your covenant and mercy with those who love You and observe Your commandments."*[1]

Nehemiah's opening words express the delicate balance in understand- ing that tunes our hearts with God's. He extols God's greatness and His mercifulness at once and together; the enormity and the tenderness of God is viewed simultaneously.

We need to grasp this balance.

It's wise and righteous that we always keep God's grandeur, His majesty and His awesomeness in view. But it's also wise to always keep the objective for doing clearly in view. Opening our prayer with a dec- laration of the majesty of God's throne is not for the sake of making theological incantations. God doesn't need to be reminded of His greatness: we do. So bringing prayer that begins with praise unto the Almighty is neither to cultivate a theology nor to affect a certain abject humility, as though God wanted to be certain we were sufficiently impressed or intimidated by Him.

Instead, praise exalts His greatness and calls my attention to my own limits—personally or circumstantially. Viewing and extolling the enor- mity of our Father can quickly settle the issue of our confidence.

Suddenly, we're standing in renewed amazement at His sufficiency to handle our need or situation!

Because He is *larger* than life, He is therefore able to handle everything about my life! our lives! The great God, so awesomely transcendent—beyond all worlds—is still within earshot of your feeblest cry. As Nehemiah said, He has a "covenant of mercy" with us—all because we have come within the covenant of His love and life through Jesus our Savior!

COMMITTED TO OBEY

I pray, Lord God of heaven, O great and awesome God, You who keep Your covenant and mercy with those who love You and observe Your commandments,...O Lord, I pray, please let Your ear be attentive to the prayer of Your servant, and to the prayer of Your servants who desire to fear Your name.[2]

Notice in this prayer the close relationship between loving God and obeying Him. The emphasis is on the heart—on the one who loves Him and is intent on doing what pleases Him. "Your servants who desire to fear Your name...who love You and observe Your commandments."[3] God honors such a desire, and hope and confidence should rise if you understand the spirit of Nehemiah's prayer. He had not attained perfection, but he prayed with a heart of obedience and God answered him.

My friend, Max Lucado, who is one of today's most loved Bible teachers, shares the story of his youngest daughter, Sara. He had just purchased a new desk for her, and because it was a piece of yet-unfinished furniture, Max was planning to have it painted before it was delivered. But Sara was pleading with him to have the store deliver immediately.

"But, Daddy," the little girl asked, "why can't we take it home?" Despite her father's patient explanation, Sara was so excited about having a new desk that she thought up reason after good reason to take the desk home that very day:

"Daddy, I'll help you carry it."

"Daddy, I just want to draw some pictures on my desk."

"Daddy, it would look so nice to have it home now."

Then was the clincher, as they moved toward the car, and her time was running short...

"It'll fit in our car, Daddy."

Max tells how he yielded to Sara's requests. He said, "I ended up doing just as she asked. Her requests were reasonable and her demeanor was respectful (no tantrums!). But most of all," Max added, "*she called me Daddy.*"

It's such a tender commentary on our human responsiveness to a warm parent-child relationship. And to suggest God is like that is not to reduce Him to a human-sized deity. Jesus said, "If you, [as entirely

---

GOD IS NOT AS CONCERNED WITH OUR PERFECTION

AS HE IS WITH OUR DIRECTION.

---

imperfect human parents] know how to give good gifts to your children, *how much more* will your heavenly Father give the Holy Spirit to those who ask Him!" (Luke 11:13, italics added).

As our heavenly Father, God honors the passion that pursues His heart with persistence joined to obedience and worship. He does this, not as a concession to our reasoning or emotions, but, as in Max Lucado's case, because of *relationship*—and because *in that relationship*, we have chosen the path of obedience—to align with His will—and are praying for what He longs to do anyway. But it also delights His heart that we call, "Abba" (Hebrew for "Daddy").

I have spoken with thousands of people who view their past and present failures as guarantees God will never be able to complete His purpose in their lives. For these people—indeed for most of us—a call to obedience seems a virtual seal against victory, for perfect obedience eludes them. But again, note the link this prayer forges between the heart and the intent to obey. What I *want* of God's will counts more than the achievement of what I've *done*.

First Samuel 16:7 says, "Man looks at the outward appearance, but the Lord looks at the heart." *God is not as concerned with our perfection as He is with our direction.* The praying heart that is intent on obedience may not immediately perfect those intentions, but God is set to respond to that one according to His "heartset."

CONFESSION IN PRAYER

We have acted very corruptly against You, and have not kept the commandments, the statutes, nor the ordinances which You commanded Your servant Moses.[4]

For God's will to be realized in my life, rather than my own, I need to be sensitized toward my sin. When I confess my sin, the Holy Spirit will help me become (a) unhooked from the clutching power of past sins, and (b) unharnessed by the sin that would seek to find present expression through me.

We have been damaged enough by sin's impact. Let us confess what we perceive as sin and ask for Holy Spirit insight to see all the more perfectly what sin may still remain in us.

I recently found myself feeling uncomfortable about a practice in my own life that I knew to be perfectly and biblically allowable. It involved my viewing habits with television. It wasn't as though I was watching impure programming. I wasn't. Nor was it that I was watching more often than before.

What was at issue, as the Spirit probed the possibilities of growth, was my recognizing a new value He was placing on my time; His call to a deeper sense of its use. I realized that it was my privilege to continue my schedule as I had: God wasn't making His saving grace contingent upon "hours not viewing." The Spirit's strong call was to reevaluate this aspect of my life, and the longer I failed to respond, the more He sensitized me to the sheer waste of "life" I was experiencing. The spent time as "sin" was not a damning failure, but I saw it as "sin" in the sense *that I was missing something better that God had for me.*

As a result of seeing the self-indulgence as "sin"—"missing the mark"—the Holy Spirit caught my attention. How often, brother, might any of us take a pure liberty granted us as believers and, by reason of attitude, turn it into a license for self-indulgence. However miscalculated such judgments on our own part may be, responding to confrontation by the Spirit and yielding to confession in prayer are keys to partnership in "building" with Him.

THE WORD IN PRAYER

Nehemiah's prayer is grounded in his understanding of the Word of God. He quotes the promises of the Word and his words are drenched in the Spirit of the Word: "Remember, I pray, the word that You commanded Your servant Moses."[5] Then he freely quotes excerpts from Leviticus 26 and Deuteronomy 4 and 28. His affirmations of God's almightiness and awesomeness are more than theological.

He is referring to a God who has manifested His power in history. Nehemiah's familiarity with the record of God's workings is at the root of his faith as he prays. He also quotes those portions of the Word that affirm God's loving-kindness and mercy.

Similarly, the Holy Spirit wants to bring the Word of God to mind as we pray. Praying "the Word" leads us beyond mere humanistic ideas about God. Praying according to the promises of the Word reminds us that it is His nature to be good, loving and merciful, so our prayer never bogs down in wonder about what God's will might be. He has revealed it. His nature is to save, to heal, to rescue, to redeem, to provide and to answer! The truths of God's Word says so, and by feeding upon it, we will soon find its truth and the faith it brings filling our praying.

BRING YOUR REQUESTS

"Let Your servant prosper this day."[6] Nehemiah specifically adds his request for royal favor when he goes to speak with the king about spending a term of duty away from the palace. He is direct in his request, but it is beautifully and wisely worth noting that the petition comes after he has taken four steps:

1. Viewed the greatness of God in worship;
2. Expressed a desire to obey God;
3. Been renewed in contrite confession;
4. Reviewed God's Word with promise.

Building with the Holy Spirit is to move into the task of personal restoration from a stance on our knees. Best of all, the Holy Spirit will assist in our *praying* as readily as in His enablement of our actions. The Spirit will help our weaknesses when we cannot know how to pray as we should.[7]

The building process will involve your complete partnership with Him and prayer as the foundational meeting point for that partnering. He will not do the job for you, but is present to help the task to be accomplished in you.

Prayer provides daily "executive planning sessions" to advance our Him-with-us building project, so open to His help. Just as the Word beckons again and again and again...*pray in the Spirit:*

- But you, beloved, building yourselves up on your most holy faith, praying in the Holy Spirit (see Jude 20).
- Praying with all prayer and supplication in the Spirit (see Eph. 6:18).
- For the Spirit helps our weakness...making intercession for us with unutterable groanings...interceding according to the will of God (see Rom. 8:26,27).

His power is ready to partner with our limitations.
Our prayer partnership with Him opens the door to it all!

SPIRITUAL WORKOUT

1. Do you find that prayer comes easily for you, or is it a struggle? If you find it difficult, why is that?
2. Can you testify to some instances of dramatic—or seemingly quite ordinary—answers to prayer in your own life?
3. What about the nature of your job/enterprise makes prayer seem either foreign or not very practical as a concept? What about your workplace situation parallels with how prayer operates? How it doesn't operate?
4. Are you aware of an aspect of obedience that you need to deal with in prayers? Is there any conscious disobedience that might block your access to the Father in prayer?
5. Does the "language" of some formal prayers in church—the

thees and thous some people use, or any other ritual habit—present any kind of a barrier to your praying in public? In private?

6. Why not close this session by having simple, brief prayers from the members of your study group, focusing especially on things the Holy Spirit is saying to them through this lesson.

CHAPTER SEVEN

What Holiness Is Really About

The Word:

Nehemiah 2:1-4

And it came to pass in the month of Nisan, in the twentieth year of King Artaxerxes, when wine was before him, that I took the wine and gave it to the king. Now I had never been sad in his presence before. Therefore the king said to me, "Why is your face sad, since you are not sick? This is nothing but sorrow of heart." So I became dreadfully afraid, and said to the king, "May the king live forever! Why should my face not be sad, when the city, the place of my fathers' tombs, lies waste, and its gates are burned with fire?" Then the king said to me, "What do you request?" So I prayed to the God of heaven.

The Target:

- To break the doubt that resists hope, whenever the idea of "holiness" creates the illusion of "impossible" in a man's mind.
- To broaden the dimensions of understanding about the idea of "holiness," giving a view of God's full-spectrumed intentions.
- To secure a man's heart in the fact of his acceptance with God in Christ, notwithstanding what of his life may still be "under construction."
- To point to Nehemiah's unselfish availability to grant the time necessary to achieve the task; noting the Holy Spirit's same availability to our "rebuilding."

What Holiness Is Really About

As often as the word "holy" is used by Christians, you would think that all agreed on a uniform understanding of its meaning. We inscribe "Holy" on our Bibles, announce plans for partaking of "holy" communion, sing "Holy, Holy, Holy" and—all in the same breath—acknowledge the "Holy" Spirit—Third Person of the Godhead. By reason of these usages, "holy" seems generally to mean "divine" or "of God."

Then, in another respect, the word of "holiness" enters a conversation—a discussion among Christians. In this context, its use may vary, from mentioning the title for a hierarchical church clergyman ("his holiness"), to listing the observances expected for the fulfillment of a ritual standard of behavioral requirements ("we are a *holiness* group of believers"). In these usages, "holiness" may mean anything from the Pope to a teetotalism regarding alcohol; from a church's bishop to not participating in entertainment on Sundays.

Then the theologians begin, and we hear "holiness" applied in a number of uses: as an attribute of God, referring to the perfection of Christ's nature, or describing the justified believer's position in Christ or the sanctified believer's manner of living. This word, in some form—holy, holiness, holiest, hallow, hallowed—occurs nearly 700 times in the English Bible. Obviously, it's important!

But what do you think it means? What does the word "holy" or "be holy" or "you are called unto holiness" suggest to you? Is "holy" something you magically "become" on Sunday at church? Can we really be "holy" in the rough and tumble of our jobs, and in our relationships with fellow workers? The target of this chapter is to answer that positively: We can! Let's talk about *how* the Holy Spirit can arrange for it to happen.

BEGINNING TO UNDERSTAND

Our understanding begins by noting that the bottom-line idea relates to something or someone belonging to God. Alone. The root concept in the Bible refers more to *being set apart* than it does the achieving of a moral perfection.

In the Old Testament, various implements and vessels used in the Temple sacrifices were described as "holy." As inanimate objects they obviously weren't "moral," but they were *consecrated*—that is, set apart for God's own use. In the New Testament, the idea of "vessels" is adapted to refer to us as God's people; in other words, we also are "set apart." (This is the meaning of the word usually translated "sanctified"—that is, set apart or consecrated to the service of God, or to be a servant of God.)

This initial look at the meaning of "holiness" or being "sanctified" could quickly bring any of us as honest believers to feelings of unworthiness (*how could I ever be that!*), until we further our understanding. For example, to read the letters to the Corinthians is to discover that they had a long way to go in their journey toward humility in character, discipline in habits and their practice of moral perfection. Still, without apology, the apostle Paul calls them, "sanctified in Christ Jesus, called to be saints" (1 Cor. 1:2).

Remembering that the root word for both "sanctified" and "saints" is the same as the root for "holy," and seeing these words applied to the Corinthians, something of hope begins to develop. Apparently you and I, as men wanting to grow in the Lord's way, can be "holy" ("saint" means "a holy one"; and as we'll see, it's a title given us "in Christ"). But first, I want to press a point home: Right there, in the midst of your job or career, even while you're still growing through and beyond the "stuff" that is less than "saintly," you can begin to learn the power of the Holy Spirit to "set you apart" as a son of the Father. Wherever your job takes you, imagine it: God has "set you there—as a distinct one of His own, *set in place for His purposes—every day.*"

Still, most of us average believers seem to feel threatened by the idea of holiness. We tend to see it as describing something of God's unapproachable side, or as demanding a quality or standard of life that is beyond us. Holiness tends to be defined by "feel" more than by fact, and the feeling seems to be, *Boy, that's way beyond me (although I sure want to try my best!).*

WHAT THE HOLY SPIRIT IS UP TO

Our study in Nehemiah's mission—nis concern, compassion and commitment to help the people—is designed to help us understand the Holy Spirit's desire to bring each of us to complete personhood. This practical pursuit—our partnering with Him as He comes to help—is geared to make us whole or holy. That's what "holiness" is really about—wholeness.

> What the Holy Spirit is up to is
> to bring the **whole** life of Jesus Christ,
> into the **whole** of our personalities,
> so the **whole** love of God
> can be relayed to the **whole** world!

The "whole idea" is "holiness." And by looking in on Nehemiah, we can gain a workable definition of holiness and grasp its practical application for us.

CONTINUING WITH NEHEMIAH

We conclude chapter 1 of Nehemiah, noting a "calling card" introduction to Nehemiah's position in the court of King Artaxerxes. We are told he was "cupbearer"—a position that was more than a mere servant, but one that at times involved a consultant role—an advisor of sorts. It was this status that gave Nehemiah his favored access to the emperor. Continuing with the text, we gain some informative insights into the customs and atmosphere of an ancient royal court.

Remember, Artaxerxes is no mythological figure. He was one of the most powerful rulers of ancient time; a pagan monarch ruling the 127 provinces of the Persian Empire, which stretched from the border of China on the east to the Mediterranean on the west, including Egypt and Asia Minor. The privilege and power of such sovereigns often manifested in impulsive and unpredictable behavior—in flights of passion and bursts of fury. So, while Nehemiah was a sort of confidant to the king, we can also understand his fear when King Artaxerxes inquired so bluntly as to the reason for his sadness.

Custom required that anyone allowed in the king's presence radiate his/her sense of privilege. But Nehemiah was still burdened with Hanani's report from the west. His grief over the condition of Jerusalem and its inhabitants, joined to his extended period of fasting with prayer, appeared to have been so preoccupying that he was guilty of violating the accepted courtroom protocol.

"Why the frown?" Artaxerxes demanded, noting his cupbearer's gloom. Nehemiah's instant response combined three beautiful traits: practical sensitivity, bold assertiveness and spiritual wisdom.

- He pacified the king: "O King, live forever!!" (*A most judicious greeting when the present possibility is the lopping off of your head!*)
- He presented his case: "My forefathers' city is wasted." (Artaxerxes would, of course, have known Nehemiah was referring to his people's capital city of Jerusalem.)
- He offered a quick, quiet prayer to God (which is a good example of the scriptural propriety of brief, pointed, emergency prayers that "find grace to help in the time of need").

The ensuing conversation resulted in Nehemiah's assignment to the task of rebuilding Jerusalem's walls. But before we study the significance of all that the king commissioned and provided for, look at the passion that motivated Nehemiah. As we search this book's unveiling of the Holy Spirit's will to work in building our lives today, there's something about Nehemiah's exchange with the king that reflects a beautiful fact about the Holy Spirit's nature, concern for and commitment to us.

The whole of this passage—beginning with Nehemiah's response to Hanani's report, to his intercession and tears, through to his risking his life in allowing his deep, troubled concern to be seen in the king's presence—unveils the character of a person who cannot be content until those he cares for are satisfied—until their purpose and destiny are "on-line," being fulfilled.

This trait is at the heart of the nature of God.

If anything summarizes the meaning of the Holy Spirit's mission to earth, it is His reflection of the Father's desire that everyone come to know the life and the love He has opened for the whole world to share. Though it is God's holiness that man's sin has violated, it is also God's holiness that sent His Son—and His Spirit—into the world to achieve His desired purpose for us all. That holy purpose is to redeem and to restore—*to wholly recover and rebuild*—just as we see Nehemiah's concern for complete reconstruction.

Nehemiah's words to Artaxerxes were neither demeaning nor

mocking toward those inhabiting Jerusalem. Though long before they should have launched the task of rebuilding, instead of faulting the Jerusalemites before the king, he showed understanding for them. He was already passionately praying, and we will shortly see how fully ready he was to offer everything he had to transform their condition.

In this passage, the character of the Holy Spirit shines forth—the true Spirit of God's *holiness.* Nehemiah wants something done—something achieved and completed for the subjects of his concern. He would prefer it be done *now,* but realism requires acknowledging that it will take time. And it is in the light of this tension—between the *now* and the *later* of God's working His plan in our lives—that we are drawn to think about the meaning of God's call to complete "holiness"; His desire for our full "sanctification."

What do those words mean, really?

We need to arrive at some conclusion on that matter, because both terms—holiness and sanctification—are too often misunderstood. They seem to have either become smothered in religious verbiage or suffocated by humanly legislated programs of "our church's rules" standards. To get beyond the encrustation of *human demands* around the idea of holiness in order to understand *God's desires* about the subject, some of us have to dismantle a considerable body of unscriptural presuppositions. We need to untangle twisted talk about "holiness"!

Because holiness is a goal God has for you and me, and because full sanctification is something He calls us to and wants us to truly desire, we must understand His reasons for it. Neither of us is likely to truly hunger or thirst for a "passed-on" quality of "pretendlike" godliness. And, if we feel intimidated by our own sense of the impossibility of "meeting standards," or have our minds shot through with a distorted definition of something wonderful about our Father's plan, wholehearted responsiveness lags. So let's investigate the meaning of "holy."

In detailing the three-part nature of man—spirit, soul and body—we earlier read Paul's prayer for the Thessalonians:

> *Now may the God of peace Himself sanctify you completely; and may your whole spirit, soul, and body be preserved blameless at the coming of our Lord Jesus Christ.*[1]

In the very words of that same prayer are three statements about sanctification or holiness. It's helpful and encouraging to note that holiness, or full recovery of spirit, soul and body...

1. Is for now;
2. Is something God will do Himself in us;
3. Involves peace, completeness and wholeness.

In short, God's program of sanctification means He is ready to do everything He can to put me fully together today!

This prayer holds a tremendous promise: "May the God of peace ...sanctify you." The essential idea of the word *eirene* (Greek, "peace") is unity; of fragments or separated parts being brought together. The relevance of the promise is obvious, whether we are viewing Jerusalem's broken walls or observing someone with a broken heart. Into both scenes a Comforter has been commissioned and committed to bring wholeness from brokenness.

THE IDEA OF "HOLY"

The full and releasing idea in God's program for our becoming "holy" deserves our best understanding. Perhaps it would help just to see how our own English word "holy" came into use. As we use it today, "holy" has been derived from the medieval English *hal*, an eleventh-century word which is the root to such contemporary words as "health," "hale," "whole" and "holy." Noting this fact helps us capture the conceptual meaning of "holiness": to see that it is broader in meaning than simply as a spiritual attribute. It relates to all of life—to the daily grind, not just to the invisibly lovely or perfect. "Holiness" involves the entire, broader idea of *wholeness*—of **completion** in all parts of the human being. Take all three aspects of "you," for example:

- Your spirit can be revived to life in God (made holy).
- Your soul can be restored in mind and emotions (made whole).
- Your physical body, habits and conditions can become disciplined and recovered to well-being (kept healthy).

Holiness becomes a far more practical and desirable goal when seen in the light of its fuller meaning. And the Bible is clear that all of these things are God's objective in making us holy. He isn't merely trying to produce stained-glass people or plaster-cast saints who are merely wind-up robots designed to satisfy some religious criteria. Rather, God wants us to become holy—that is, complete in all our being—just as He is holy, or complete in Himself.

HOLY AS HE IS HOLY

Let's take the phrase, "be holy as He is holy," because what to many of us may appear to be prohibitive summons or unattainable goal is actually a verse that gives us a great glimpse into the Father's heart and desire for us.

It is in the book of Leviticus that this high call is initially issued: "For I am the Lord your God. You shall therefore consecrate [sanctify] yourselves, and you shall be holy; for I am holy."[2] For years that verse caused me to shudder with a dubious, reverential fear. As I read, I knew I was accountable to its summons, but I also felt that it held an obviously impossible challenge.

Compounding my sense of concern, and deepening my fear of failing, I noted Jesus saying essentially the same thing: "Therefore you shall be perfect, just as your Father in heaven is perfect."[3] Here, I thought, is an Old Testament and a New Testament summons calling me to be perfect. With that thought, a near-paralyzing sense of helplessness and hopelessness would possess me: *I want to be what you want me to be, Lord, but it all seems so out of my reach.* It was there that a divine call intended to beget hope produced fear and condemnation instead. I never really gained ground on the subject until, through one simple moment of understanding, that futile sense of being a "failure before you start" was broken.

Before we go any further, can we establish that? If the walls of your personality are going to be rebuilt, I want to assert that you too will be best advanced toward that goal by coming to the same place of comfort and confidence that God's Word gave me. Let me elaborate.

TWO KINDS OF HOLINESS

I know of nothing that hinders the pursuit of holiness more than a sense of condemnation.

Guilt.

Feelings of worthlessness.

Doubting the possibility of *ever* being truly satisfying to God.

These all war against faith and hope. But when we discover the two ways holiness and perfection are revealed in His Word, both faith and hope can be rekindled. The knowledge that we are "called unto holiness" becomes infused with promise instead of defused by condemnation.

———

BY THE STANDARDS OF THE HIGHEST COURT

IN THE UNIVERSE—WE ARE AT ONCE DECLARED,

"NOT GUILTY—HOLY!"

———

Clouds first begin to brush back from the soul when the foundational ground is cleared of confusion, giving a place for godly confidence to stand. First, the Father invites us to see how our holiness is initially secured before Him: It starts with the *position* He gives us in Christ.

The Bible flows with grace at no greater point than in its disclosure of the way that God, by virtue of a person's choice to put his faith in His Son Jesus Christ, *declares* that person "Holy!" In other words, the instant when you received Jesus as your Savior, you were placed in a new "position" in your standing with God. The Epistle to the Romans repeatedly uses the word *justified* to describe this action. It's a giant of a concept—a word meaning that God, the Judge of all mankind, has made a legal judgment about you and me. When we trust in Christ, He not only declares us "holy," but He also gives His legal reasons for doing so. Because we are putting our trust in the righteousness of Christ instead of our own achievement, God puts the sinless record of His Son as a credit to our account.

He not only removes the record of our guilt, but He also enters the record of Christ's absolute sinlessness! It's astounding and amazing— unquestionably the grandest show of grace we could imagine!! And so it is, with Jesus' sinless record credited to our account, *now*—by the standards of the Highest Court in the universe—we are at once declared, "Not guilty—holy!" With the flawless record of the Savior superimposed over our failures, God announced us as, *"Wholly holy!"*

Second, after so graciously securing our *position*, God's Word talks about holiness in *practice.* He wants us to get on with a life that is *lived* "holily," which practices holiness in thought and conduct. This means that as newborn children of His, He is looking for growth—and practical holiness is that. It isn't a matter of improving our status with God, but of verifying the reality of His work which has begun in us.

Don't miss this: While we're growing, in the meantime we are fully accepted because of our "positional holiness" (through Christ). Keep that in view, because God means for that point of understanding to sustain our sense of peace and assurance in His love, while we're growing. But at the same time, keep it equally clear: The Father won't allow us to neglect responsible growth in practical holiness on the grounds that we are already positionally holy. I can't beg off my call to follow Him obediently as a growing disciple by whistling "Amazing Grace" as though that were an argument for my right to self-indulgence.

It was when I learned to see and to balance these two facts that fear, doubt and guilt were broken, and I was allowed to see what the Lord Jesus meant when He said, "You shall be perfect, just as Your Father in heaven is perfect."

I had always seen these words as a commandment—a *demand,* if you will. The words seemed like a shout, insisting, "You better shape up, because God's watching!" But one day it dawned on me: These words aren't a command—they're a *promise!* Jesus was saying something about the holy genetic of God's own seed—His nature, which the life of His Spirit brings into us and is prepared to grow up in us.

Just as someone might say, "It looks like you're going to have brown eyes because your Dad does," so Jesus is saying, "Because your Father is holy, that quality of His own person is destined to increasingly become evident in you. Give place to it!" Let me even further elaborate how vividly the *real truth about holiness* can bring hope to our hearts!

TWO STEPS TO CONFIDENCE

I am convinced that there are two steps that will give any man a settled confidence that God can make him holy:

- Step One: To understand holiness in **God's changeless nature**;
- Step Two: To understand His promise about **your new nature**.

First, let's take time to talk about *holiness* as it applies to God. By theological definition, "holiness" is defined as, "that attribute by which God preserves the integrity of His own being." Simply put, that means that His "holiness" is the very part of God's nature that insures everything else about Him will never be reduced.

"Holiness" refers to His absolute "completeness"—a quality that totally removes Him from the category of any created being or thing. By reason of His "holiness," God's love is never less, His faithfulness can never be greater, His truth is always trustworthy, His purity will never be compromised, His judgments are unswervingly fair, etc. God never needs to be reminded to be good, loving, wise or wonderful. He never has nor ever will need to say, "I think I'll be nicer today," nor "I hope I don't do something evil by accident." In other words, He doesn't labor to accomplish that which most of us define as "being holy."

And that is what is behind the reason that holiness conveys the root meaning of "being set apart"—that is, in a category of its own. That's why teachers sometimes say God's holiness means He is "the utterly *other* One"—separate, apart from and beyond. It explains Isaiah's words when he caught a sense of the presence of the Holy God: "I saw the Lord *high and lifted up!*" In seeing this part of the meaning of God's "holiness," it is right that we be captivated by the *grandeur* of His Person. But at the same time, never lose sight of the *grace* that His "holiness" guarantees us.

Because He is holy...

- God will never be without love for you.
- God will never be less than merciful.
- God will never be other than just.

The greatness of His holiness assures us that He will never be anything other than what He is by the glorious essence of His perfect being. His "holiness" preserves that, and the whole perfection of the completeness of His Person will always be the same.

SO IN THAT LIGHT...

In the radiance of all we have just discovered, let's look at *man—* "mankind" in general—*man* as "human," or *man* as you and me.

In stark contrast to the completeness of God, man now stands as "incomplete"—that is, "damaged property, reduced in quality from the original product"—*unholy*. But remember, this wasn't the way we were created.

First created in God's *holy* image, but now *unholy* as the result of the Fall, *man* has been shattered and smashed—impacted by the loss of so much we were initially made to be. Created "complete"—that is, "holy"—we had a potential for living life "completely"—never coming up short, missing the mark or functioning at less than full capacity.

The story of the human dilemma is that without a reborn human, reconditioned by the renewing work of the Holy Spirit, humankind cannot possibly find its highest fulfillment or richest fruitfulness. "Unholy" is more than a stamp of failure on our faces, it is the word that describes our loss of that which alone could produce completeness in our lives.

"But God..."

It is here, at this point of our helplessness to change anything, that God's saving, healing, freeing love and grace enter the scene. He sends His *holy* Son to die for our sins and **redeem** us; then He sends His *Holy* Spirit to fill our lives and **restore** us! His plan unveiled: He has set forth a *holy power* to birth humankind all over again, then, by this "new birth" to sow into human nature a new seed—a new, restoring genetic principle making possible "wholeness" (i.e., the completeness, the "entirely other than I would be otherwise," of "holiness").

This is what the apostle Peter means when he says, we are "born again, not of corruptible seed but incorruptible, through the word of God which lives and abides forever" (1 Pet. 1:23). Go ahead and repeat those words again: let the implication massage its way into your soul, because you may need as much time to "get it" as I did.

Even though this promise in God's Word declares the certainty of this "new seed" potential in our lives, my own disposition toward focusing on my limited "works" rather than God's unlimited "grace" got me stuck in a point of miscalculating the greatness of His promised power toward me as a *son*.

Reading 1 John 3:6,9 disturbed me. It says:

> *Whoever abides in Him does not sin. Whoever sins has neither seen Him nor known Him...(but) whoever has been born of God **does not** sin, for His seed remains in him; and he **cannot sin**, because he has been born of God"* (emphasis added).

I would read those words and be ready to give up—to throw my hands up in futility and ask the question, Am I really "born of God!"? My thoughts would run like this: *Well, I **think** I'm born of God, but this says if you are you don't sin, and sometimes I still do. I don't want to, but I do. I mean, I love the Lord and I'm trying to become more holy, but I still sin.*

With this, the words of verse eight would haunt me: *He who sins is of the devil,*[4] and it was too easily that the spirit of doubt and con-

---

ONCE I HAVE BEEN BORN AGAIN, I'M RUINED FOR

BEING THE KIND OF SINNER I WAS!

---

demnation would try to make a playground of my soul. A kind of futility would creep around the edges of my mind: *Since I'm not sinless yet, am I really saved?*

For years I would come across this verse and wrestle with the questions it brought. Like others I've known, I made repeated trips to altars and prayer rooms, hoping to assure that my failures weren't sealing a doom I hoped my salvation had released me from. But one day I learned that the verses that had confused me by seeming to breathe doubt were actually given to stimulate faith. They contained a blessedly beautiful and awesomely mighty truth, which corrected my misunderstanding when I discovered the simple fact of the Greek verb tense in those verses.

Can you imagine my joyful sense of release—the hope for eventual holiness!—when I saw that the original language actually says, "Whoever is born of God *does not keep on sinning*"! The words were not meant to say a new believer is rendered unable to sin again, but that the life of God in you and me assures that *we are on a path of growth that is relentlessly reducing our capability to sin as we have in the past!* In a very real sense, this passage of Scripture says, "Once I have been born again, I'm ruined for being the kind of sinner I was!" *Hallelujah!* This understanding helped me to see why, only verses before in the same epistle (1 John 2:1,2), the words of the apostle call to a balanced perspective: Pursue holiness, but receive forgiveness when you fail...

> *My little children, these things I write to you, so that you may not sin. And if anyone sins, we have an Advocate with the Father, Jesus Christ the righteous. And He Himself is the propitiation for our sins, and not for ours only but also for the whole world.*[5]

We're told, "Don't sin...but if you do, His blood is your covering!"

What a truth for all of us who say, "Father, I want to walk in Your holy way, but sometimes I struggle still with sin!"

The message is clear: The seed of God's new life in me assures me that my destiny is to conquer sinning, and His life in me will make me unhappy when I sin in ways I have in the past.

How often, before you knew Christ, did you sin and feel justified in doing so? Remember feeling free to retaliate, to let your temper flare or to serve yourself selfishly? Now, have you noticed since your rebirth that an inner sense of discomfort with sin and a desire to please God has begun to predominate?

Your answer is the same as mine: "Absolutely, *yes!*"

And there is a reason that we experience a greater sensitivity about sin and a deeper longing for His holy will prevailing. *We've been born of God!* His seed remains in us, and He's saying to us, by His Word and by His Spirit, "I have birthed My life into yours. What isn't like Me doesn't fit anymore, and who is like Me is moving to take over!" Let me illustrate.

Everyone who knows or has seen me knows that I have a receding hairline. (Actually, I *used* to have a "receding" hairline: *now I'm bald!*) Naturally, as you can imagine, I did not plan to become bald. In other words, in my early twenties I didn't make a calculated decision to begin losing hair. But I did begin losing it. And if you knew my family, you could have predicted I would, because both of my grandfathers, as well as my dad, had precisely the same hairline. It was inevitable that I would lose my hair, because the same gene that caused their loss was in me! A principle that caused them to be balding was transmitted to me.

Now it may seem a less than worthy analogy, but in that simple fact about my *biological* genes, I'd like us to see something God says about your and my *spiritual* genes. Our growth in "holiness" may take time, but it is not going to be a humanistic struggle at becoming religiously perfect. Instead, the Holy Spirit—get it, the *HOLY* Spirit—has come to progressively restore the Father's intended image in me. He has come to fill my broken, weak and damaged parts, and in doing so, to bring about the character and constancy of my Father—whose seed is in me, as His child. Let's rejoice, brother!

ON BOARD FOR THE DURATION

Then Nehemiah said, "Send me that I may rebuild," to which the king replied, "How long will your journey be?"

"And I set him a time," Nehemiah reports. He registered his request,[6] and do you know for how long? One of the most moving things in this whole book is to discover what he said, for though the words aren't here, we learn from reading, **Nehemiah asked for 12 years!**

Can you imagine it!?

I can imagine a man—in the comfort of the palace and the security of his position, saying, *I'd like to take a two-month leave of absence;* or *Well, King, sire—May I have permission to be there—well, could I possibly have a year?*

But *12 years!*

Yet the analogy is beautifully appropriate, for just as Nehemiah recognized the task would not be accomplished rapidly, the Living God knows the same about you and me. And He has sent the Holy Spirit—with great loving-kindness and *mercy that endures forever*—to work with patience toward bringing His full restoring work in us. Even when it takes more time than we thought, God has sent the Holy Spirit to come on board our lives for the full duration of His program geared to work His will in us!

And just as that ancient king agreed, so God Almighty has declared His willingness to grant the time needed for growth: "The Lord will perfect that which concerns me; Your mercy, O Lord, endures forever."[7] Whatever time it takes, the Holy Spirit is committed to our completion—to "holiness" in our lives.

He will provide the power. He simply calls for our willingness to partner with Him—and participate in what He directs.

SPIRITUAL WORKOUT

1. What is the popular perception or definition of a "saint"? How has this chapter redefined that perception with biblical definitions?

2. Are conditions or situations at your workplace or in your career making it difficult to remember that you are called to be "holy," or "set apart for God's special use"?

3. Can you accept the affirmation in this chapter that the nature of God is not to be content until those He loves are fulfilled in His purpose?

4. God is portrayed in Scripture as both "high and lifted up" and able to dwell in the lowliest of hearts (see Isa. 57:15). Is your own main concept of God weighted toward perceiving Him as totally "other" from man, or as a companion and friend?

5. What positives in accepting, or negatives in over-emphasizing, can you see in the idea of "positional" holiness before God?

6. Interact with someone about your response to the development here of the biblical idea that God's "seed is in you, and you cannot sin."

PART TWO

DIMENSIONS OF DEVELOPMENT

Jerusalem's walls, how can it be
I see your stones arise?
If this can be, then surely thus
can God restore our lives.

Come, Holy Spirit, have Your way,
O Comforter Supreme.
Rebuild my soul, redeem all loss,
fulfill my highest dream—
My Father's purpose.

—J.W.H.

CHAPTER EIGHT

BUILDING SUPPLIES AND PROJECT PLANS

The Word:

Nehemiah 2:4-9

Then the king said to me, "What do you request?" So I prayed to the God of heaven. And I said to the king, "If it pleases the king, and if your servant has found favor in your sight, I ask that you send me to Judah, to the city of my fathers' tombs, that I may rebuild it." Then the king said to me (the queen also sitting beside him), "How long will your journey be? And when will you return?" So it pleased the king to send me; and I set him a time.

Furthermore I said to the king, "If it pleases the king, let letters be given to me for the governors of the region beyond the River, that they must permit me to pass through till I come to Judah, and a letter to Asaph the keeper of the king's forest, that he must give me timber to make beams for the gates of the citadel which pertains to the temple, for the city wall, and for the house that I will occupy." And the king granted them to me according to the good hand of my God upon me. Then I went to the governors in the region beyond the River, and gave them the king's letters. Now the king had sent captains of the army and horsemen with me.

The Target:

- To see the adequacy of God's provision for the accomplishing of the "building project" represented in each of us.
- To affirm the distinction between this "building project" and our initially coming to Christ: a contrast represented in Israel's two separated experiences of divine deliverance—from Egypt and from Babylon.
- To reassess the strong "material" in our "foundation" as we open to Christ as our Savior; then to see what supplies are needed for effective building on that foundation.
- To study the biblical basis for our authority in Christ, over and above the powers of hell; to see how the Holy Spirit wants to deepen our convictions regarding this practical issue in growth.

BUILDING SUPPLIES AND PROJECT PLANS

What is needed for the building of a man or the rebuilding of broken parts of the personality? How is the job contracted? What materials are needed? Are there permits to be issued, as a city code might require for a projected structure?

These aren't merely rhetorical questions; they're essential ones. Answering them will sharpen our sense of the need for rebuilding the real you, and for reenergizing the Body of Christ in general and God's men in particular.

This is not a hobby, but a real and urgent project. It will take real time and will require real materials. As Nehemiah requests of the king a leave of absence from the court, the reality and practicality of planning for reconstruction unfolds in our text.

Artaxerxes is as quick to respond favorably to Nehemiah as he was quick to show displeasure over Nehemiah's despondency. Apparently God answered Nehemiah's prayer. The king immediately changes his demeanor and he and the queen willingly hear Nehemiah's request. And all the more moving—especially in light of our comparative study—is to see the evidence of Nehemiah's forethought and preparedness.

He is ready for the occasion.

He instantly seizes the opportunity and makes his requests known. He has planned carefully for this moment, and in his specific requests we are provided insight into principles that help us find the best answer to the questions: What is needed to rebuild a personality? What does the Holy Spirit need to rebuild the Body? In the basic things for which Nehemiah appealed, truth unfolds from which these questions can be answered.

Nehemiah requests and is given four things as he obtains the right to pursue the Jerusalem rebuilding project. They are:

1. Time—an extended period of leave from his duties at the palace;
2. Authority to enter the region of activity;

3. Resources for the actual building project;
4. Troops to secure his mission and support him in the event of opposition.

As men, we have a special opportunity—and obligation—to accept responsibility for allowing the Holy Spirit to guide us into productive use of each of these resources. Conventional wisdom finds many of us protesting, "But I don't have time....If I only had the authority....I lack the ability....I just don't have the resources." The fact is that each of these resources are creations of the Living God. And from Creation, God has empowered man to "subdue" and "have dominion over" the created order for His glory. We are free to exercise dominion over time and resources and authority to bring about personal and corporate renewal.

But before we examine the nuggets of truth in these four gifts, let's take a minute to assure that one preliminary issue is settled. It involves an important distinction in personal spiritual experience.

Bondage and Captivity

In discussing the process of restoration in the human personality, we need always to distinguish rebuilding from rebirth.

You have probably been born again already. Your interest in this book is probably but one evidence of your sincerity and desire to grow as a Christian. But I have wondered if another possibility might be the case for you. Can it be that as you have been reading, you have become aware of something unsettled in your own soul? A longing, perhaps, that seeks an established confidence about your personal relationship with God?

If this is so, it is further possible that until now you have never actually come to a specific moment in your life when you asked Jesus Christ to be your Savior. Have you ever personally invited Him into your heart?

We all need to do so, you know.

Jesus said that unless we come to God in humility as children, we cannot truly begin in the life of God's Kingdom.

> *Assuredly, I say to you, unless you are converted and become as little children, you will by no means enter*

the kingdom of heaven. Therefore whoever humbles himself as this little child is the greatest in the kingdom of heaven.[1]

Let me ask you, gently but pointedly: "Have you ever done that?"

Have you knelt humbly as a child and confessed your sin to God with childlike honesty? Have you prayed with childlike simplicity, inviting Him as the young child's song requests,

> Into my heart, into my heart,
> Come into my heart, Lord Jesus?[2]

If you haven't until now, then would you now join me in doing that? Just pray—simply, quietly, but speaking these words with sincerity:

Holy Father God,
Depending on Jesus, I come to ask Your
    forgiveness for all my sin.
I want Your will in my life and Your Word as my
    guide.
Thank You for giving Your Son for my salvation:
    I now believe in and receive Him as my Savior
    and as my Lord.
      I receive Your love given to me
        through His death on the cross, and
        I receive Your life given to me
          by His resurrection from the dead.
Lord Jesus Christ, come into my heart.
Fill me with Your Holy Spirit,
  and let all my tomorrows increase in Your way
    from here to eternity. Amen.

Let's pause a minute. Whenever the moment that transaction between you and God occurred, whether just now or years ago, let us stop right here and praise God together!

The fact of Christ's entry into our lives is an ever-present reason for praise. You and I have *great* reasons to lift our voices with praise full of thanksgiving. Here are just seven!

1. *All our sins are forgiven completely!*
   God says, "Their sins and iniquity I will remember against them no more."[3]

2. *Complete peace with God has been established!*
   "Being justified by faith, we have peace with God through our Lord Jesus Christ."[4]

3. *The courts of heaven resound with joy because of our salvation!*
   Jesus said there is joy in heaven over each sinner who repents.[5]

4. *Our names are now written in the Book of Life!*
   It is an actual registry in which God has listed all of us as His redeemed.[6]

5. *We have an absolute hope of eternity in heaven!*
   "The gift of God is eternal life through Jesus Christ our Lord."[7]

6. *Christ promises His daily presence and provision!*
   "I will never leave or forsake you...I have come to give life abundantly."[8]

7. *God has committed Himself to help us resist evil!*
   "And if God is for us, who can be against us?...We are more than conquerors through Him."[9]

Rejoice and praise with great thanksgiving! Go ahead and do it!

Lift your head.
Lift your hands.
Lift your voice.

New life in Jesus Christ is yours forever, and these seven facts are only a few of the multiple guarantees you have from God—promises which secure confidence for your future. And it is beautifully assuring that hereby God's Word gives firm footing for tomorrow. Whatever yet needs recovery, you have a solid and sufficient foundation in Christ. Here are grounds for rejoicing and upon which you can progress with rebuilding!

Two Distinct Points of Beginning

Pausing to insure your foundation in Christ is important simply because without our rebirth, rebuilding is an impossible task. Without secure footings through faith in the death and resurrection of the Lord Jesus, any attempts at building or rebuilding a life are destined for frustration and failure. "No other foundation can anyone lay than that which is laid, which is Jesus Christ."[10]

However, once our *beginning* is secured in Christ, *building* can be effectively pursued. It is therefore not surprising that the Bible delineates so clearly between foundations and rebuilding. In a real sense *both* are a beginning, but each is distinct and needs understanding. Thus, God's Word not only teaches two distinct points of beginning, but there are Old Testament parallels to illustrate each of the two.

The initial beginning point is regeneration: "You must be born again."[11] We've just outlined that point at which the foundation is laid. It is virtually instantaneous, because everything about it has already been accomplished for us through Christ's death and resurrection: we are saved completely by His grace and His work[12] and secured in the power of His perfected salvation for us.[13]

The second beginning point is sanctification:[14] "He who has begun a good work in you will keep performing it until the day Christ returns for you."[15] This is a progressive program of growth and involves our responsible partnership with the Holy Spirit. It includes the Lord's promise to restore to us all that we have seen lost or destroyed in our past.[16]

So the two points merge. When the initial "beginning"—rebirth—is established, we're ready for the second—rebuilding. Look at the examples in Israel's history. On two ancient occasions the Jews found themselves troubled by circumstances in lands distant from their Promised Land of God's intended purpose.

The first was their sojourn in Egypt. After Jacob's family relocated, during his son Joseph's influence there, later rulers reversed what had been a benevolent setting. The Israelites' situation progressively deteriorated until later generations were put under slavery. Centuries later, under Moses, came their exodus, when the Lord delivered them, saying: "I have brought you out of Egypt, out of the house of bondage."[17] Through the miracle of the Passover and the mighty display of their passage through the Red Sea, they were liberated; a nation resurrected from death.

The second occasion was their exile in Babylon. Following Jerusalem's destruction, the Jews were made political captives—a displaced people "marking time" as it were. But when the quota of prophesied years-of-judgment was fulfilled, the Lord brought them back, returning them to the land of their inheritance and the city of their former rule.

Now there is a vast and obvious difference in these two experiences. It's an instructive difference, much like the distinction between regeneration and sanctification—between being reborn and being rebuilt.

For example:

1. In *Egypt* they were slaves under brutal taskmasters. In *Babylon* they were refugees, but with the opportunity of carrying on somewhat of a normal enterprise.
2. In *Egypt* their slavery was simply the result of their heredity. After successive generations, each one was simply born into bondage. In *Babylon* their exile was the direct result of sinning which produced their situation. They were a destroyed and displaced people.

Furthermore, the pathway to release in each case was different:

- Deliverance from Egypt came through the blood of the Passover lamb.
- Return from Babylon came by means of the king's edict, according to the prophecies of God's Word.

The relevance of contrasting Israel's Egyptian bondage and Babylonian captivity is that the rebuilding process we are studying parallels the outcome of the latter event—their return from exile. That must be clearly seen because we should never suppose a person's new birth is a process—it isn't.

Our rebirth in Christ is a crisis, a moment in time when, like Israel's deliverance from Egypt, the blood of "the Lamb of God who takes away the sin of the world"[18] is acknowledged. That is our only hope of freedom from sin.

But following this we will all come to that time when we begin to deal with the fruit of past disobedience, in the same way Israel's exiles returning from Babylon had to face the charred remains of Jerusalem—the direct result of past sinning.

First, the Lord Jesus Christ comes as Savior—the only solution to our deadness in sin, our lostness from and our guiltiness before God. His cross is the key to our redemption and His resurrection power the key to our receiving the gift of new life in Him.

Second, the Holy Spirit comes as Comforter—the One sent to assist us in our helplessness, to instruct us beyond our ignorance and to recover us from all our brokenness. His power is promised us and His leadership given to assist us forward in our new life for Christ. He comes with all the equipment needed for our rebuilding, renewing and recovering.

Some thrilling analogies to our experience are highlighted by an analysis of the text before us.

THE NEED FOR LETTERS OF AUTHORITY

Furthermore I said to the king, "If it pleases the king, let letters be given to me for the governors of the region beyond the River, that they must permit me to pass through till I come to Judah."[19]

Analysis: Each of the Persian Empire's 127 provinces was ruled by a satrap—a provincial governor charged with protecting the emperor's interests and the empire's boundaries. Customs were due, passports required, documents checked and the usual requirements of at least a cursory investigation of all travelers was administrated. In Nehemiah's case there was an unusual need for evidence of his mission and commissioning, for upon arrival he would be functioning under a special order of the king's court. Although his mission would not completely displace the regional governor's authority, it would alter its dimension. Insofar as the Jews and Jerusalem were concerned, Nehemiah was invested by Artaxerxes with a higher authority than Sanballat, the satrap over the region. Nehemiah was governing with direct authority from the emperor. His request for documents indicating his right of passage and privilege of rule are understandably requested. It would greatly expedite the task if there were no questions as to who's in charge.

———

THE PRIVILEGE OF PRAYING AND OPERATING IN THE NAME OF JESUS ARE THE LETTERS OF AUTHORITY PRESSED INTO YOUR HAND BY CHRIST THE KING.

———

Analogy: When Jesus ascended to heaven, He had expressed at least two promises of far-reaching significance: (a) He would build a Church and (b) He would give the Church authority to act in His Name.[20] He further made clear that the Holy Spirit's coming would provide the power to accomplish the task of building and the ability to exercise the power of His Name.

And the Holy Spirit has come!

As participants in His building process, we need to understand the authority the Spirit has brought us. The Comforter wants us all to utilize the letters of authority we have been given: "Whatsoever you ask in my name," Jesus said, "the Father will do it for you."[21] And "All authority has been given to Me in heaven and on earth."[22]

These credentials—the privilege of praying and operating in the name of Jesus—are the letters of authority pressed into your hand by Christ the King. The Holy Spirit will teach you to function in those rights as well, and this is a significant point of learning because we are all a people living on a planet under contest.

Since man's fall, the Adversary, like a Persian satrap, is ready to claim authority unless we can verify higher claim. And that's what we have been given in Jesus' name. We not only have throne rights of *access* to God, we have throne rights to *advance* Christ's kingdom IN HIS NAME!

Just as Sanballat's authority over Jerusalem and its residents was pre-

empted by Nehemiah's letters,[23] so the Holy Spirit has come to enforce
the King's orders concerning you. Whenever the devil seeks to drop a
pall of gloom over you, distressing you with a spirit of heaviness—
whenever he seeks to encroach upon the present workings of God's
purpose in your life—drive him off the property: "You have no authority here! In Jesus' name I declare my right to freedom and privilege of
pursuing God's project in my life!"

MATERIALS FOR THE PROJECT

*And a letter to Asaph the keeper of the king's forest, that
he must give me timber to make beams for the gates of
the citadel which pertains to the temple, for the city wall,
and for the house that I will occupy.*[24]

Analysis: The crucial need for wood in the ancient day cannot be
appreciated by today's building standards. So many varied construction
materials are now used, and steel is so commonly utilized for frames
and beams in large structures, that we can easily miss the significance
of Nehemiah's request. He needed the large timbers for structural
framework. They would be absolutely essential for the completion of
the project.

Notable, however, is the fact that the vast majority of the material
to constitute the rebuilt walls would be the stones that were already
on the site. They would use tons of rock—some stones still the shape
originally quarried and others broken beyond apparent use—but all of
it remaining debris of the former walls.

Analogy: In the conjoining of these two materials—new beams and
old stones—there's a picture of God's redemptive program which
restores broken people like us. First, there are always things that God
must bring to our recovery. Paul seems to hint at this supply-line ministry of the Holy Spirit in his letter to the Philippians:

*For I know that this will turn out for my deliverance [sal-
vation] through your prayer and the supply of the Spirit of
Jesus Christ....My God shall supply all your need.*[25]

The Holy Spirit's *supply* is foreshadowed in Nehemiah's request for those materials that must be brought to the task; those "timbers" of God's resource for renewal that He is more than ready to provide.

But, like the broken, fallen stones of Jerusalem's wall, there are also things present within you which, though battered by the past, can be readied again for building. There are traits of your own unique personality, memories of your own past, qualities of your own character—distinct hallmarks of YOU—that God wants repaired and retained: "For it is God who works in you both to will and to do for His good pleasure."[26]

These two resources provided by Nehemiah—authority and materials—forecast the method God is using to equip us by the ministry of His Holy Spirit today:

1. The Adversary is confronted with our badge of authority: Jesus' Name!
2. The task is approached with sufficient resources: a renewing supply of divine grace and a redeeming power to recover building blocks from broken pieces.

And with all of this, as the text describes, Nehemiah was given a cordon of soldiers—another mighty point paralleling the Spirit's ministry to us.

Let's explore in the next chapter the intriguing question of what those soldiers represent today.

SPIRITUAL WORKOUT

1. Weighing the elements of promise in the Holy Spirit's readiness to provide the *time, authority and resources* for building or restoring matters in your life, what response do you offer? Patience, to match His? Trust, to receive His strong correction? Peace, in receiving His strong protection? What resources do you feel you need to open yourself to receiving from Him?

2. Do you have a settled and peaceful sense of having initially escaped the bondage of sin through the grace of God, or are there lingering doubts about your salvation and the presence of the Holy Spirit in your heart?

3. Nehemiah needed "letters of authority" as passports and supply requisitions in order to rebuild the walls of Jerusalem. On a sheet of paper, write your own "letter of authority," allowing the Holy Spirit to inspire your heart with a sense of His personal attention to those issues that will need to be faced as you are being built/restored. (Example: "From the Living God, before all powers of this world or the realm of darkness: I hereby declare my authority is engaged to bring (John Jones) to the realization of....")

4. This chapter notes the authority Jesus gave the Church to act in His name. Discuss your sense of what this means, and your relative confidence or comfort with this authority.

CHAPTER NINE

A BAND OF ANGELS

The Word:

Nehemiah 2:9,10

Then I went to the governors in the region beyond the River, and gave them the king's letters. Now the king had sent captains of the army and horsemen with me. When Sanballat the Horonite and Tobiah the Ammonite official heard of it, they were deeply disturbed that a man had come to seek the well-being of the children of Israel.

The Target:

- To grasp a scriptural view of angels, and the part they play in "ministry" in behalf of believers.
- To recognize that learning to perceive the reality of the invisible realm of spiritual activity is not a move into superstition or into a mystical mind-set, but rather to learn to function as a biblical believer, in the power of the Holy Spirit.
- To identify some of the tactics employed by our common Adversary, the devil, in order that we may more readily draw on the Word of God and the ministry of the Holy Spirit to resist him.

A Band of Angels

The beloved spiritual intones, "Swing low, sweet chariot...a band of angels comin' after me,"[1] and sentimentalizes on the presence of angels at the time of death. "Bands of angels" *are* mentioned in the Bible. Jesus said that, at will, He could have summoned a host of them to rescue Him.[2] But the angels of Scripture are neither playful cherubic dolls nor "chariot" attendants at death. Even though the Bible has much to say about angels and their role toward us, a dearth of teaching about them exists.

Some have so reacted to superstitious ideas about angels that they seem to take exception to the truth on the subject. But religion's hangover from medieval traditionalism is no threat when we heed the Word.

Paul wrote to the Colossians, "Let no one defraud you of your reward, taking delight in false humility and worship of angels."[3] His warning not to become preoccupied with the subject of angels is soundly in view, but it was never intended to remove us from an understanding of their activities. There are, in fact, as many references to angels in the New Testament as in the Old—almost 300 in all! So let us address the theme wisely, giving an appropriate emphasis to a subject that can be as imbalanced by neglect as by preoccupation.

ANGELS AND YOU

First, Hebrews 1:14 says, "Are they [angels] not all ministering spirits sent forth to minister for those who will inherit salvation?" That's an extremely important verse because it pointedly assures us that angels are not merely winged wonders flitting around in the sky, but are ministering spirits appointed an explicit task. They are assigned ministry toward "those who will inherit salvation."

Now the Bible makes clear who this is: We are salvation's heirs, all the redeemed in Christ. Romans 8:16,17 says, "We are...heirs of God and joint heirs with Christ." And in Ephesians 1:11 we read, "In whom [Christ] also we have obtained an inheritance." It is no exaggeration of the Word to accept the fact that included in the vast benefits and promises of the great inheritance God gives us, He has provided the attending ministry of angels. He has sent "a band" of them to assist us and to work at His direction in our behalf.

Remember the Acts 12 account of Peter being freed from prison? An angel loosed him from his cell and caused sleep to fall on the guards.[4]

Remember in Acts 8 when Philip left Samaria to go to the desert to meet a man in need? An angel told him to do that.[5]

Remember in Acts 12 when Herod (after he killed James), smugly arrogated authority to himself and suddenly dropped dead under divine judgment? An angel struck him down.[6]

Remember in Acts 27 when Paul was storm-tossed aboard the ship bound for Rome and he urged all on board to take heart because God assured him of their safety? An angel delivered that message to him.[7] "Are they not all ministering spirits sent forth to minister for those who will inherit salvation?"[8]

The biblical answer is yes! These are clear New Testament cases of angelic agents assisting people of the Kingdom with deliverance, guidance, comfort and judgment.

Yet someone might say, "Those cases are certainly true and quite remarkable, but those things just don't happen today—except, well, in some Communist country or something." But the eternal Word declares, "For He [the Lord] shall give His angels charge over you, to keep you in all your ways. They shall bear you up in their hands, lest you dash your foot against a stone."[9] Angels have the ministry of *protecting*; that's at least one of their assignments.

Most of us can point to times when something unexplainable suddenly happened—imminent disaster was averted or remarkable deliverance effected. And all of a sudden we recognize it—the Lord sent help! Some of the most phenomenal stories I've heard in my life, miraculous stories of invisible but obvious assistance, are apparently the activity of angels. Intellectualism taunts those who suggest the possibility of contemporary angelic action, but it isn't fanatical to believe such things occur. We might well let the Word open our eyes to see.

Most of us see into the invisible realm with great difficulty. But more activity occurs there than some suppose. In 2 Kings a marvelous story involving angels is told.[10]

During the time of the prophet Elisha, the king of Syria sent a large military contingent of horses and chariots—a great army—after him. When Elisha's servant saw the enemy surrounding them he cried out, "Alas, my master! What shall we do?" Elisha's calm response has become a classic quotation: "Do not fear, for those who are with us are more than those who are with them."

The wise old prophet not only knew he had divine protection—he *saw* it. When his servant responded by saying, "I don't see any troops on our side," Elisha prayed, "Lord, open his eyes that he may see." And God opened the servant's eyes to see that "the mountain was full of horses and chariots of fire all around Elisha."

Haven't you experienced a similarly surprising insight into a larger dimension of reality? Even in a man's world of work, numerous examples of these experiences can be cited. A salesman sets a goal and reaches it, then another and another, until, looking back, it's hard to believe how far he's come. "I didn't know I had it in me," he may say. Maybe he doesn't! Maybe a protective angel is arranging contacts with prospective clients, entrusting the man with more material means so he can enjoy the blessing of blessing more and more people.

Or a church reaches a certain level of ministry, and the pastor calls for another level of outreach. Attendance booms because so many more people are finding their needs met. Yet the sum total of ministry seems greater than the individual parts (members). Are the people to say they did it on their own, or is it not possible, even probable, that God honored their commitment to the next level of ministry by sending ministering angels to help?

This promise is yours as well. God provides *accompanying* care as well as the protective, the liberating and the ministering work of angels. Just as He did for Paul and his companions in the storm, He has "sent forth [angels] to minister" for us.

The captains of the army and horsemen that accompanied Nehemiah beautifully parallel the ministry of angels in the life of the believer. They aren't to be sought or worshiped, but they have been assigned and we needn't fear acknowledging their activity. Just as armed troops accompanied Nehemiah from the palace in Shushan, so God, in pouring His Holy Spirit upon the Church, has also bequeathed provisionary troops—the hosts of the Lord, a band of angels to assist us when need arises.

THE FALLEN ONES

But this is only one side of the coin. In stark contrast to the angelic hosts serving the Father's purpose are dark powers aligned against us: "For we do not wrestle against flesh and blood, but against principalities, against powers, against the rulers of the darkness of this age, against spiritual hosts of wickedness in the heavenly places."[11] Sanballat's opposition to the efforts on Jerusalem's walls reflect the satanic, tyrannical nature of our Adversary, the devil, who is set against our wholeness:

> When Sanballat the Horonite and Tobiah the Ammonite official heard of it, they were deeply disturbed that a man had come to seek the well-being of the children of Israel.[12]

Sanballat was the provincial governor over the realm of Judah and his control had been absolute. Previously nothing could happen without his approval. But now one fact overruled that: Nehemiah had brought official letters from the emperor putting the Jews in Jerusalem under Nehemiah's authority. He had been given the right, if he wished, to annul anything Sanballat said. It was the one hope that these citizens had for realizing the restoration of their city walls.

Now we read that this spiteful ruler *grieves* that a man has come from the king to help these oppressed and needy people.

Think about it! It is so characteristically satanic!

Sanballat's only interest is to keep the people in a state of defeat and despair, for his sole purpose is to secure rule over them. He exacts taxes from them, concocts demands of them and exploits their weaknesses. He is completely disinterested in the well-being of these he has been charged by the government to serve. Sanballat's spirit is as accurate a picture of Satan as you will find anywhere in Scripture.

FACTS ABOUT THE DEVIL

The prophets Isaiah and Ezekiel both speak about the fall of Lucifer.[13]

Under the configuration of the *prince of Tyre*, Satan is identified as a sinister being, destructive in every design, hideously hateful and opposed to all that is God's purpose and desire.

In Genesis he is introduced as the *serpent* in the Garden, the same title that follows him into the book of Revelation where he is also called the *dragon.** He is primarily referred to as "Satan" (meaning *accuser* and *adversary*) and "the devil" (meaning *slanderer*). The Bible reveals that Satan is a spirit being who was originally created in beauty and perfection by the hand and breath of God, but who rebelled against the Most High. Still, as a created being, he is finite in his capacities, though he transcends the power of mankind in our present estate.

Though he is a formidable adversary, Satan is not omnipotent, however great his power. Only God has all power. And Satan is not omnipresent—only God can be everywhere. Through demon hordes, which like an evil army serve at his direction, the devil seeks to strategize and execute his master plan—a program formulated to deceive and destroy individual persons and the whole race of mankind as well.

It is important to know these facts about the devil, for contrary to the notion that he is only an abstract force, a negative way of thought or an impersonal expression of evil, the Bible gives a different picture. God's Word reveals him as a distinct, vile personality who rules the forces of darkness and operates systematically in the spiritual realm against everything good, righteous, noble, pure and healthy.

SATAN IS OUR ADVERSARY

Just as Nehemiah knew how to deal with Sanballat by leading the Jews in resisting his efforts at hindering them, we need to let the Holy Spirit's message in the Word unmask Satan's person and methods.

First Peter 5:8 calls him our adversary and teaches us to "be sober, be vigilant; because your adversary the devil walks about like a roaring lion, seeking whom he may devour." Some sincere believers are intimidated by such words and prefer to simply skirt the subject and pretend their enemy will leave them alone if they do the same with him. But that idea is unjustified. The Word says he is stalking us. So let's learn the truth about him and allay all fears. Concerning Satan's powers, certain reasonable questions rise.

First, how broad is Satan's arena of action? The God we worship and the Christ who redeemed us both created and rule the entire universe! Satan's scope of power is only on this planet, earth. That may be small comfort, however, since this is where we live and his assault seems unavoidable. But before we faint or tremble, remember it is also to this

———

NEW BIRTH PLACES EACH OF US OUTSIDE SATAN'S
REALM OF RULE, EVEN THOUGH WE CONTINUE TO
LIVE ON THIS PLANET WHERE THE BATTLE STILL
RAGES FOR HUMAN SOULS.

———

small planet that God has sent His Son and announced, "All authority has been given to Me in heaven and on earth."[15]

When Jesus offers the privilege of being born again into God's Kingdom, the fact is that new birth places each of us outside Satan's realm of rule, even though we continue to live on this planet where the battle still rages for human souls. Perhaps it will help us to grasp the nature of this battle if we understand its history, for man was not originally placed on earth in this dilemma.

How did Satan gain rule over this planet? According to the Bible, God created our planet for man's governorship under God. But through deceit and disobedience, man believed and obeyed the serpent's lie. He listened to the snake, disobeyed the Creator, and thereby, Satan has come into controlling management of the earth—a role originally intended to be man's. The devil still exercises this rule by "just rights," having received license to this rule through man's disobedience to God and his forfeiting his God-given rule to Satan.

We know the devil has legal claim to function on earth, for when he offered "all the kingdoms" of this planet to Jesus, attempting to seduce Him to sin, Jesus did not contest the devil's right to make that offer. He did rebuke the temptation, but He didn't correct the tempter's right to make the proposition. Thus, the struggle goes on to see man's rule reinstated under God. So, understanding the history of the battle, the next logical question is:

What license does Satan have to operate in my life? The entire life of a person outside of Jesus Christ is lived under the sway of the prince of the power of the air, "the spirit who now works in the sons of disobedience."[16] In other words, an unregenerated person is not only still in his sins because of Adam, but he is also completely vulnerable to the dominion of the Adversary by reason of living in his domain.

This certainly does not mean that every unbeliever is demon-possessed. Nor does it necessarily mean that non-Christians even consciously or willfully serve Satan. But it does mean that man's whole thought system, his whole pattern of life and conduct, is far more motivated, animated and manipulated by the Adversary than he understands. The whole world, the Bible says, is under the influence of the Evil One.[17]

And how shall I recognize and respond to Satan's workings? There are several traits of his activity. *Satan is a liar,*[18] but you don't have to respond to the lies of the Adversary. *He is an oppressor,* but you don't have to let him oppress you. Keep Acts 10:38 in mind: "How God anointed Jesus of Nazareth with the Holy Spirit and with power [to deliver]...all who were oppressed by the devil." That's just one of the sure promises we live in as the same Holy Spirit is present to help us!

Satan also infects hearts and minds with evil. Jesus likened the Adversary to a sower of evil seed that grows into a weed-filled garden,[19] who directs activity sowing things opposing God's goodness in your life. He further seeks to steal the good seed of the Word of God when it comes to you. He will resist faith-inspiring promises and fruit-bearing seed,[20] but you can counterattack by clinging to and declaring God's Word of truth! Don't let the thief succeed at stealing, killing or destroying.[21]

Now to summarize these satanic traits:

- He lies.
- He imposes fear.
- He depresses.
- He sows doubt.
- He seeks to defeat and discourage.

Where good things have begun, Satan will seek to abort what God's

Word is working. When the Word does gain a foothold, he seeks to snatch it away. As your enemy, he'll seek to wipe out any and all hope of holy, joyous expectation.

But remember that although we live on the scene of this conflict and face these devilish devices, don't allow that fact to suggest surrender. You have your rightful place in God's promise and victory! Our Nehemiah has come with letters of authority that overrule our opponent and preempt his authority over us!

Truth will overthrow his lies.

Deliverance will cast out his oppressive works.

The work of grace will weed out what he seeks to sow.

Anything that opposes you has an answering counterforce in God's Word, and the Holy Spirit will stir your mind and warm your heart and faith. Though the thief comes to steal and destroy, the Holy Spirit will rise with Christ's abundance of grace so that your restoration and growth can go on: "When the enemy comes in like a flood, the Spirit of the Lord will lift up a standard against him."[22]

Victory is *yours! Now!*

And yet I have sometimes felt the soul-wearying hostility of hell wearing me down. Amid the struggle I have felt low at times, even though I knew I was destined for triumph beyond the test. If you've ever felt like that, wearied though you're winning, maybe this story will help you as it has me.

PLAYING "AWAY FROM HOME"

When I played basketball in high school, on one occasion we were playing "away"—playing a game on another school's home court. Our team was playing quite well—outscoring the opposition, in fact—but somehow the sense of winning just wasn't there. Our momentum began to fade.

Recognizing the problem, our coach called "time." As we huddled at the sidelines, he began: "Hey guys, listen up. You're *winning.* But I know it just doesn't 'feel' like it. Now brace yourselves. Understand this. You're playing on 'enemy territory' and you've got little crowd support."

Because of the distance, few of our high school's kids were there. The crowd was made up of opposing fans. Every time we'd score, we heard nothing but boos. Whatever the other team did was lauded and applauded, and though we were ahead, a horrible sense of being defeated hung in the air. The coach recognized its effect on us, and having wisely helped us see the source of our "lag," he sent us back into the game.

We won.

And so it is in the middle of some trying situations. The Adversary opposes you. You're in God's will and purpose, but sometimes feel depressed: "It sure doesn't *feel* like I'm winning!"

But cheer up, Teammate!

Don't let the Adversary's crowd of demon liars get you down. You may not have the home-court advantage at this time, but you do have the presence of a Coach who wants you to remember, "He who is in you is greater than he who is in the world."[23]

Yes, Sanballat will continue to prove to be a hatefully accurate picture of Satan. And in Nehemiah, we will further see a very tender picture of the Holy Spirit confronting evil and advancing the recovery process. In helping you withstand the Adversary, the Holy Spirit further assures you,

- "I'm going to get you together."
- "I'm going to rebuild you."
- "I'm going to restore you."

Dear one, there's overcoming confidence in perceiving the real nature of the spiritual battle. The enemy and his company are real, but so is the conquering Comforter and His heaven-sent troops.

Everything Satan can do can be overruled by the present ministry of the Holy Spirit in you. Let the Holy Spirit make the letters of authority in God's Word alive to you and in you. Overrule the devil and stand in the certainty "that He who has begun a good work in you will complete it until the day of Jesus Christ."[24]

I may be uncompleted, but I'll never be defeated.

SPIRITUAL WORKOUT

1. The original meaning of the Greek term for "angel" was messenger. Name two important events in the life of Christ when an angel filled this role. (See Luke 2:8-14; Matt. 28:1-8.)

2. Have you come to terms with the reality of the fact that angels are active in the world today?
3. Have you ever experienced an instance or instances when you believe divine protection or provision came to you by reason of angelic activity?
4. Beside instances when angels may be appointed to our defense by the Father, what other means of protection from Satan does the Christian have? (See James 4:7.)

CHAPTER TEN

BREAKING LOOSE FROM CONDEMNATION

The Word:

Nehemiah 2:11-15

So I came to Jerusalem and was there three days. Then I arose in the night, I and a few men with me; I told no one what my God had put in my heart to do at Jerusalem; nor was there any animal with me, except the one on which I rode. And I went out by night through the Valley Gate to the Serpent Well and the Refuse Gate, and viewed the walls of Jerusalem which were broken down and its gates which were burned with fire. Then I went on to the Fountain Gate and to the King's Pool, but there was no room for the animal under me to pass. So I went up in the night by the valley, and viewed the wall; then I turned back and entered by the Valley Gate, and so returned.

The Target:

- To show that Nehemiah's work on the walls of Jerusalem builds our confidence in the Holy Spirit's work of restoring the soul.
- To encourage patience during "dark times," and when God doesn't seem to act immediately.
- To affirm that God's restoration of your soul frees you from being dominated by guilt and a painful past.

Breaking Loose from Condemnation

Talk about *incredible!* I just heard about a pastor who "preached him-self out of the ministry!" It's no joke. And sad as it is, so truly it occurred—this way.

Chuck (the name I'll use for the story) had been an alcoholic before he was converted. He knew he was no worse a sinner than, say, the apostle Paul. He also knew in his head he had been forgiven by the boundless grace of Christ. Yet he could not experience this fact in his heart; he could not forgive himself. Each time he preached about sin, his own sinful past would unreel before his eyes. Finally, in despair, he resigned his ministry.

Somehow, Chuck was unable to internalize one of the most tender and lovely verses in the Bible from Psalm 23: "He leads me beside the still waters. *He restores my soul.*" This faithful and gentle description of our Savior's ministry is but another reminder of God's purpose to *restore*—to recover whatever remains wounded or broken in us. This next piece of history Nehemiah describes provides mighty truth that unmasks another adversary to our fullest development: condemnation.

Few experiences are more crushing than this feeling of perpetual reproach. As in the case of this minister, the soul-wrenching power of condemnation has proven how emotionally and mentally crippling it can be. It wipes out one's sense of God's peace and plays havoc with faith's underpinnings. But Jesus' loving attention, as our soul-restoring Good Shepherd, wants to lead us beside the streams of Holy Spirit-inspired truth and the liberating rivers that can dissolve the chains condemnation has forged.

Nehemiah's restoration work in Jerusalem is so representative of the way the Holy Spirit begins His restoration work that it's unsurprising so many vivid analogies occur.

Before the city was destroyed by King Nebuchadnezzar, the ancient city of Jerusalem had 10 gates. Nehemiah mentions in 2:11-15 visiting the ruins of three of these ways of access through the city's walls: The

Valley Gate, the Refuse Gate and the Fountain Gate (see diagrams in chapter 5). The purpose of this tour, which Nehemiah took before anybody even knew why he had come to Jerusalem, was to explore the actual condition of the walls. His survey enabled him to determine where he would first need to concentrate his efforts.

Nehemiah's report noted that as he proceeded, he finally came to a place where he could go no farther. The destruction years before had been so complete that the rubble blocked his passage at every turn. He specified a point on the severe eastward slope where the ruination made it too dangerous to advance any farther. He turned back and reentered the city by way of what remained of the Valley Gate—the point he had earlier exited. Nehemiah's survey report gives both a sense of the devastation and an appreciation for the enormity of the task he faced.

We are studying actual events in history and yet we discover in them so many devotional analogies. Types break forth everywhere, picturing redemption and showing how the Holy Spirit works today. As we trace this man's survey of ruins, notice the phrase, "after three days." It's the first of several points at which you'll find parallels quite helpful in breaking free from condemnation's quest at quenching the joy of the Lord in your soul.

Analysis: Nehemiah's arrival at Jerusalem was followed by three days of virtual inactivity. There was no fanfare, no high celebration, no announcement of intent. The passage of time was doubtless a practical one of adjustment, of his getting settled following the arduous demands of so extensive a trip. These days would also have provided time for thoughtful consideration of his first steps, now that he had actually reached the scene of his mission.

Analogy: How often have you wondered why God doesn't do things more quickly? Because impatience with God's "waiting periods" is trying for the most mature, how much more is it true of those who have yet to learn that the coming of the Spirit rarely includes an immediate change of circumstance?

Throughout the years I have had many ask, "Pastor, since I've been filled with the Holy Spirit, I *feel* different but it doesn't seem like much else *is* different." They go on to note how a week...two weeks...a month has passed, and they're concerned that dramatic events aren't filling their days "like all those other people" they've heard testify.

I usually seek to comfort them with two facts:

1. My experience with dramatic testimonies is that they are honest, but usually abbreviated. People report, in condensed version, things which took much longer in coming about. Don't feel like a second-class Christian when time seems to be passing by and action seems slow.
2. God is never in a hurry. Yes, the presence of the Holy Spirit within us does bring an instant witness; He's there and He's at work.[1] But remember this: The gifts and the fruit of the Spirit aren't unwrapped with haste or grown at a moment's notice. If things aren't happening fast, you're normal.

The relevance of our learning to recognize that God's delays are not denials is that such understanding can defuse the tendency to feel unworthy—condemned—simply because things aren't happening as fast we think they would if we were "more acceptable" to God.

Analysis: Nehemiah makes a triple reference to his nocturnal tour investigating the condition of Jerusalem's walls.[2] He was not yet ready to tell the people his plan, nor was he interested in the provincial government's knowing his purpose. So under the cover of darkness, silent in their exit and quiet about their task, a small group of men traversed the devastation caused by a disaster occurring a century and a half before. Even as the people slept, unaware that long-sought help had come and lifelong embarrassment would shortly be overcome, Nehemiah went about his task, dedicated to their interests.

Analogy: How apparent the Scriptures are that God is always awake and alert, tending to our need: "The God of Israel never slumbers or sleeps"[3] and "I lay down and slept; I awoke, for the Lord sustained me."[4] His Word indicates that even while we are at rest, our Father's program for our blessing is being sustained. As surely as your heart is kept beating through the night, His heart concern for you is being carried out.

Sometime back, through the death of a family member, I was moved to do a study on God's activities "in the dark." I was amazed at the number of major events in the Bible that brought victory in the midst of darkness:

- Creation's light sprang into the darkness of chaos (Gen. 1).

- Jacob wrestled all night and gained a new identity (Gen. 32).
- Israel's Passover deliverance took place in the night (Exod. 12).
- Gideon's battle unto victory began in midnight hours (Judg. 7).
- The scene at Jesus' cross was immersed in inky blackness, though it was midday (Luke 23).
- Even when Jesus comes again it will be as a thief "in the night" (1 Thess. 5:2), and during an era of history predicted as one in which "darkness shall cover the earth and deep darkness the people" (Isa. 60:2).

This truth can bring such bright exhilaration to the soul! The Holy Spirit is ministering to your need now. Whatever the apparent darkness, God "never forsakes the work of His hands."⁵ Rather than allowing depression or the darkness of waiting to become a shadow of doubt, or letting a cloud of questioning cause you to believe yourself the victim of God's apparent inactivity, learn this wisdom:

> Dark times are intended for your rest. When they come, lean back and recline in the everlasting arms of the Almighty. Allow the Holy Spirit to work *out* and *through* what He's surely at work doing.

I guarantee: When morning comes you'll be surprised!

LESSONS AT THE VALLEY GATE

Analysis: Nehemiah's survey team exited at the Valley Gate passageway from Jerusalem. This gateway, like all the others, was now only a worn path, not a structure. It seems more than coincidental that this is the first point of reference.

Interestingly, the Valley Gate derives its name from its view upon and access to the small, narrow Valley of Hinnom (see diagrams in chapter 5). Long before Nehemiah's visit and far earlier in Jerusalem's history, the Canaanite people had worshiped there. Human sacrifices had been offered as their satanic ritual was pursued.

Later in history, at a time when the Hebrew prophets confronted

Israel for involving themselves in the same evil rituals, blood and death still stained and shadowed Hinnom. Eventually the people were judged and exiled for reasons including the fact that some had sacrificed their children in this very valley. It had been a shrine of Baal, the damning cult that defied God's laws and pled the evil case for perversion.[6]

Thus the Valley of Hinnom became known as the Valley of the Flame or Fires; a place where human sacrifices had been offered. Even when this period passed, Hinnom continued to be used as a place for burning rubbish; a fact prompting this valley's adoption as a symbol of

---

YOU NEVER NEED TO ACCOUNT FOR THE PAST AGAIN!

---

forthcoming horror. Both in the book of Revelation, as well as in Jesus' preaching, Hinnom is used to describe an ultimate site of eternal damnation. Gehenna (a form of the name Hinnom) is that awesome, awful lake of fire.

Analogy: Clearly, the Valley Gate's prospect is a ready and logical picture of hell, for it depicts the prospect of a life outside Christ, with neither hope nor meaningful destiny. And it is not profane to observe that one's present life, if outside of God's will, can be "a hell of a life"—hellishly self-centered, hellish in its activity, hellish in its fruit and hellish in its destiny. What the Valley Gate represented from Israel's past is symbolized in our study. It's the point where the worst of the past is seen and where it is dealt with conclusively.

VALLEY GATE—LOOKOUT TO THE PAST

That Nehemiah's first survey exits from the Valley Gate parallels the Holy Spirit's desire to start by begetting in us a personal sense of our past having been dealt with. His invitation to you and me is: "Stand at the doorway of your life and look on your past. Its future was eternal loss. Just as the Valley Gate faced the western, sunset side of the city," the Spirit continues, "see yourself secured in Christ's forgiveness—the sunset declaring an end to that segment of your life."

Standing at Jerusalem's gates, in confidence that yesterday has concluded, brings a fresh certainty concerning my tomorrows. On the cross Jesus declared, "It is finished!" confirming the completeness of all salvation. Now the Holy Spirit makes it personal: "Whom the Son sets free is free indeed."[7] You never need to account for the past again!

THE SERPENT WELL

Analysis: The viability of the Valley Gate's being analogous to the securing of our souls is highlighted by the fact that nearby this gate was the Serpent Well. Nehemiah mentions it, and it is still marked today.

Scholars say the Serpent Well was named in the way folk names have always been ascribed to geographic sites today. Just as Indians and settlers have given such names as "Devil Mountain" or "Snake Creek" for logical or superstitious reasons, the Serpent Well was probably named for the fact that a snake had been found and killed there at some time in the past.

Analogy: The image is graphic: A thirsty man seeking water is attacked by a snake coiled at the well. The snake is slain and the man's thirst slaked. In this beautiful picture we can hear Christ say, "Whoever drinks of the water that I shall give him will never thirst. But the water...will become...a fountain...springing up into everlasting life."[8] Thirsty souls respond. Yet, just as the Serpent would seek to prevent access to this joy, so the Son of God has risen to smite the Serpent's head. And now He calls us to drink endlessly at the well of salvation's joy.[9] In Nehemiah's starting through the Valley Gate and coming to the Serpent Well, envision a picture of the Holy Spirit wanting to bring us to:

1. A place of security about our past;
2. A place of victory over the devil's efforts at depriving us of the daily joy of our salvation.

The Holy Spirit would say, "I want to bring you to a well where you will drink with joy, and rest without fear; where the serpent is pressed under your feet and because of my dominion in your life, You are no longer subject to accusations of the liar concerning any aspects of your past sin and failure."

Steadfast confidence in your relationship with God is basic to feeling confident about the future. The Holy Spirit wants to help you with this. If God was sufficient to cover your past, when you were dead in sin and lost from His purpose, He can handle your future now that you are one of His own.

Break free from condemnation!

Whenever the enemy accuses you, learn to resist his efforts in the resource of God's truth. Stand your ground on what God has spoken about your sins:

> If we confess our sins, He is faithful and just to forgive us our sins and to cleanse us from all unrighteousness (1 John 1:9).

> As far as the east is from the west, so far has He removed our transgressions from us (Ps. 103:12).

> Who is a God like You, pardoning iniquity and passing over the transgression....[You] will again have compassion on us, and will subdue our iniquities. You will cast all our sins into the depths of the sea (Mic. 7:18,19).

> "Come now, and let us reason together," says the Lord, "though your sins are like scarlet, they shall be as white as snow; though they are red like crimson, they shall be as wool" (Isa. 1:18).

> "I have blotted out, like a thick cloud, your transgressions, and like a cloud, your sins. Return to Me, for I have redeemed you" (Isa. 44:22).

> Then He adds, "Their sins and their lawless deeds I will remember no more" (Heb. 10:17).

That last verse, which quotes from Jeremiah 31:34, declares one of the mightiest possibilities in the universe. God forgets sin. "Their sins and their lawless deeds I will remember no more." He means this! It is not a case of senility or forgetfulness, but of divine eradication. He completely removes our sin record from His memory. In other words,

God says, *"Because my sinless Son's record of righteousness is now applied to you, and because I have no instance of sin to recall about Him, I can't think of anything you've done that displeases me!"*

That's what being justified means. We are acquitted of any grounds for judgment. We now stand with Christ before the heavenly tribunal and the Almighty Father God, Judge of all, says, "I have superimposed my Son's record over yours. Now I regard you as never having sinned. Your past is abolished from my memory."

Live in this confidence, loved one. Rejoice in condemnation-free living.

And the next time the devil comes to remind you about your past, remind him about his future!

SPIRITUAL WORKOUT

1. Are there any "shadows" of guilt that reach from your past into your present? Any incidents you would feel willing to share with your small group? Prayer can break the back of residual condemnation, and may also be applied to rebuke the spirit of condemnation that so often delights to keep us in those "shadows."

2. Even without sharing specific sins of the past, the group may want to participate in a simple exercise to impress on your minds the fact of Christ's forgiveness. After each one writes a past sin on a small piece of note paper, crumple the notes and (safely) burn them; at the same time, recalling Jesus' words, "It is finished!"

3. Read Revelation 12:9,10. Who is called "the accuser of our brethren," and what other traits does he have?

4. Have you ever come though a period of "darkness" and discovered that God was tending to you even when you weren't aware of it? Rehearse this, with praise—or, share it with your small group.

5. Go back and review the six highlighted verses clustered in the section titled, "Breaking Free from Condemnation." Write these references in the back of your Bible, or some other place for frequent or timely reference as a weapon against recurrent accusations of the Adversary.

Two Gates and A Miracle

The Word:

Nehemiah 2:14-16

Then I went on to the Fountain Gate and to the King's Pool, but there was no room for the animal under me to pass. So I went up in the night by the valley, and viewed the wall; then I turned back and entered by the Valley Gate, and so returned. And the officials did not know where I had gone or what I had done; I had not yet told the Jews, the priests, the nobles, the officials, or the others who did the work.

The Target:

- To encourage patience and confidence with those issues that hinder our growth, and which seem to take so long in being resolved. To recognize the Holy Spirit is working, even when it seems "dark" to us.
- To point to an expectation of "breakthrough," with a trust in the Holy Spirit's plans for victories along the way to our ultimate triumph.
- To see Jerusalem's ancient Dung Gate and Fountain Gate as a picture of our need to see a restoration and maintenance of practical confession and cleansing, joined to the purifying power of the Word of God.

Two Gates and A Miracle

The power of Jesus to heal instantly is an intriguing part of the stories faithfully recorded in the Gospels. Yet there is a little story in Mark's Gospel that is, to me, equally intriguing because Christ's touch resulted in a healing that came in two stages.

A blind man was brought to the Lord to be healed. Jesus led the man away from the crowds and actually spit on his eyes and laid His hands on the man. Then He asked if the man saw anything.

"I see men like trees, walking," the man said.

Can't you imagine what the man thought? "Is this my miracle? I was led all this way in hope of restored eyesight, and all I have is a blur?"

Or, on the other hand, was he so happy to be able to see *anything at all*, he might have been willing to settle for the blur! Well, we don't know his thoughts, however distressed or satisfied, but what we do know is that Jesus *finished* the job! The second time He touched the man's eyes, they were fully restored to sight, and he saw everyone clearly.

Like that man, do you sometimes wish everything happened at once, and that there were no "blurs" in the process of God's restoring or rebuilding you to complete wholeness or maturity? Do you ever get impatient with such stages of healing in your own life? My friend, Lane Adams, has succinctly expressed this feeling in the title of his book, *Why Is It Taking Me So Long to Get Better?*

Amazing numbers of believers seek miracles to resolve the problems that cripple their progress. They want Jesus to speak an immediate word: "Rise and walk." How we would all like our growth and rebuilding to be accomplished with but a word. Yet the Savior says instead, "I'm going to teach you to walk rather than cause you to, for far greater things are learned when you discover a walk with Me and not just a miracle from Me."

This process is much like the natural one by which a child learns to walk. It begins with the child's natural desire to want to get up—to gain a beginning capacity to stand on its feet. Next he will learn to move about while still holding on. Then, having learned healthy balance, he eventually steps forth, to the joyous delight of the whole family.

Miracles are involved in our learning to walk in the life of the Spirit of God, but they aren't completely essential to that walk. There are basics we must start with and then, at times, miracles will follow. But first steps are usually slow in coming, and the miracles are joyful moments rather than a continuum of phenomenal events.

When our oldest son was born, his feet pointed almost directly outward. At first we all thought this would gradually remedy itself. But by the time he was beginning to scramble around and pull himself to his feet, nothing had changed. As he began to walk it was with difficulty. He could not walk well and there was sufficient cause for us to take him to the doctor for attention and treatment. For months special shoes were placed on him and it appeared the next step was leg braces, for still no improvement occurred.

This is one of the most precious stories in our family's history, and my wife Anna tells it best. She had just left one doctor's office for another. The first, who had been caring for little Jack, had recommended the baby be fit with braces and given therapy by an advanced specialist. Anna had just boarded the bus en route to another specialist that morning and, with the baby in her lap and her hands grasping his feet, she simply prayed, "Lord Jesus, you know how much I would like this little boy's feet to be all right."

That was the entire prayer! Yet minutes later, as she disembarked from the bus and entered the next specialist's office, they both looked with astonishment at our son's feet—they were perfectly straight! What months in remedial shoes had not changed had been rectified by the touch of Jesus in 15 minutes! They were both dumbfounded with delight, and you can imagine the praise session Anna and I had together as we laughed and rejoiced over the genuine miracle of the instant recovery of our little boy's foot condition. What long-range implications for his future!

We still rejoice when relating that episode. It was real, unimagined and given by God's grace. And I tell it here because within it is a principle about our learning to walk in the Spirit. Young believers, like young children, *do* have the capacity to stand, the ability to get around *and* the desire to move forward with balance. But we all need a miraculous dimension of life in order to truly move forward—to run the race of a Spirit-filled life.

These "first steps" and a miracle outline the text of Nehemiah. With the two steps in the last chapter, three more are discernible from Nehemiah's first excursion. They depict further foundational points for moving forward in a Spirit-filled walk—the steps following the joy of finding condemnation-free living.

DEALING WITH SIN

Analysis: Older translations called this the "Dung Gate," a name it bears to this day in modern Israel. Of course the titling of a portal using the word for human excrement is admittedly distasteful. But the fact is that daily, the city's garbage was removed through this gate and that refuse included human feces—plain old piles of the unnamed, except for the polished-up Bible word—dung!

Analogy: The Refuse Gate is clearly a picture of the purging and cleansing process every earnest believer must walk through daily. Nothing is more fundamental to a healthy walk with Christ. As completely as our past sins are forgiven and our position secured in God's grace, a need still exists for maintaining our hearts in purity before Him. Being among the first places scrutinized by Nehemiah, the Refuse Gate is reflective of the Holy Spirit's aim to keep us sensitive to sin, obedient in life and conscientious to confess our sin when we fail. "But if we walk in the light as He is in the light, we have fellowship with one another, and the blood of Jesus Christ His Son cleanses us from all sin."[1]

Say a man prays for the guidance of the Holy Spirit in his daily work. The office atmosphere is tense with sexual innuendoes or backbiting and gossip. He prays that the Spirit would be present between people at the office so relationships would be smoother, but nothing happens! Is this brother to assume that it's just not the Lord's will to send His Spirit into the office? Or is it possible that the man himself has been co-opted by an attitude—by the spirit prevailing there, and that he needs to expel that from his life like the refuse it is? Is there something he himself is contributing to the less than ideal atmosphere, something he needs to be bold enough to confess instead of denying its presence in hopes the Holy Spirit will come and "fix" everything for Him?

I have often found it difficult to talk with people about sin and their own need for being sensitive to confess and keep cleansed daily. So many individuals quickly feel utter condemnation. It seems when anything is said about sin, a giant self-destruct button is pressed and condemnation clouds their countenances. But in dealing with us more deeply to prompt holiness of life, Christ does not point out our sin to condemn us. He's revealing it so we will repent, confess and be brought to a new place "in the light." Cleansing, confidence and joy are available as the blood of Jesus Christ purifies and delivers.

This daily need for confession is similar to your body's breathing process. As you inhale, oxygen is carried to the bloodstream and

———

[THE HOLY SPIRIT] IS NOT ACCUSING—"AHA, I SEE YOU!"—AS THOUGH SOME HEAVENLY HELICOPTER IS SPOTLIGHTING YOUR FAILURE UNTIL ANGELIC OFFICERS ARRIVE! BUT HE DOES USE THE LIGHT OF THE WORD TO SHOW YOU WHERE HE WANTS TO WORK IN YOUR LIFE NEXT.

———

courses throughout your whole body. In circulation, the blood picks up impurities from cells throughout your body and upon return, the impurities are filtered through your lungs—some even expelled with exhaling. So it is when the Holy Spirit surfaces sin. He is not accusing—"Aha, I see you!"—as though some heavenly helicopter is spotlighting your failure until angelic officers arrive! But He does use the light of the Word to show you where He wants to work in your life next.

Where sin is surfaced, confession is required: "If we confess our sins, He is faithful and just to forgive us our sins and to cleanse us from all unrighteousness."[2] The combination of the Word and the blood of Jesus Christ will work their way through your whole spiritual system, beginning to purify all you'll allow. And as you confess (somewhat as exhaling in the circulation process), your confession of sin becomes the key to freedom.

The Greek word for "confession" is *homologeo*. It means, "to speak the same thing." That is, to say about sin what God is saying to you about it. Confession involves being honest, forthright and not excusing yourself either to God or to your own conscience. If the Father says, "I don't want you to do that," then respond, "Lord, I don't want to do that." If He says, "I see that you have not yet surrendered that," then say, "I see it now Lord, and do surrender it." Confession: I say what He says and the light of His Word (with the cleansing power of the blood of Christ) progressively purifies me.

The same passage in 1 John reminds us that if we say we have no sin, we're fooling ourselves. Remember, the position we have gained in Christ is not threatened. Peace is not sacrificed during this process of practical sanctification. But our total acceptance before the Father is no substitute for the fact that He is calling us to move into holiness—that is, restoration and a fuller wholeness of personality.

We *can't be* any more accepted than we already are as His children. We *can't be* any more victorious than we are in the dominion He's given us over the power of the enemy.

But *we can become* progressively purer in the practical details of daily living. To balance these truths is to move ahead. The Dung Gate is part of the program. And as disturbingly graphic as the picture is, the message is clear: Daily purging is no shame; it's healthy.

BEING IN THE WORD

The words themselves are seemingly innocuous, but the symbolism in them is profound as Nehemiah says, "Then I went on to the Fountain Gate."[3]

Analysis: Most scholars believe that the Fountain Gate was given its name because its eastward location was just above and opened to a path leading down to the Kidron Brook (see diagrams in chapter 5). It would have been the gate through which many of the people went daily in order to get water.

Analogy: The Fountain Gate seems to readily depict the Word of God. The Bible describes itself in many ways: as bread, milk, gold, honey, a mirror, a hammer and, in John 15, as water. Jesus said, "You are already clean because of the word which I have spoken to you."[4] As the people went daily to get fresh, life-sustaining water at the Fountain Gate, so it is impossible for a believer to survive apart from continuous interaction with the Word of God. If you were to ask me what a believer needs in order to move on with God, I would say that a believer needs to:

1. Know where he stands with God in Christ;
2. Know he has been given dominion over the devil in Jesus' name;
3. Know how confession of sin allows an ongoing, purifying work of the Spirit;
4. Know that he needs to be in and daily feed upon the Word;
5. Know that he is to be filled and live in the fullness of the Spirit.

The Fountain Gate illustrates the fourth point, just as Nehemiah's words, "I went on...to the King's Pool"⁵ pictures the fifth one.

BEING FULL OF THE HOLY SPIRIT

Analysis: The King's Pool resulted from a project initiated approximately 300 years before Nehemiah's time. About 750 years before Christ, Hezekiah, one of Judah's godly kings, rose to power. Among his building projects was the strategic carving of an underground conduit designed to bring a fresh water supply into the city of Jerusalem.

Until that time, whenever Jerusalem was attacked by enemies, a simple siege could reduce the people to defeat. But now, thanks to Hezekiah, the solid granite conduit brought water from the Gihon Spring outside the city walls to a pool built within the city (later named The King's Pool). It was a remarkable engineering accomplishment for any time, but all the more considering the conduit was dug 2,700 years ago! It is an interesting archaeological fact that the workers started from opposite ends and cut their way through the rock to within one foot of a precise contact.

When the King's Pool was dedicated, it meant that a continuing life-saving water supply was now within the city of Jerusalem. Some scholars suggest that Psalm 46 was penned to be sung at the celebration of that pool's inaugural: "There is a river whose streams shall make glad the city of God" (v. 4).

The King's Pool was functional in Jesus' time (and still is today!) and was called the Pool of Siloam. Remember when Jesus put mud on the blind man's eyes? He said, "Go, wash in the pool of Siloam,"[6] and the record indicates that the man born blind began *seeing*.

Analogy: The biblical record of the King's Pool gives a picture of a flow—a water supply within that:

- Helps to resist attack;
- Sustains refreshment;
- Ministers healing.

Nothing could more beautifully illustrate the purpose of being *filled* with the Holy Spirit!

As I mentioned earlier, our son's first steps were significant. But the miracle healing of his feet was the mighty, much-needed release of his walking, even *running*, into his future. Now, let me urge personal application of that message. As we have noted,

- Personal *assurance* in Christ and *dominion* over the serpent were studied as we considered the pictures given us at the Valley Gate and Serpent Well; and,
- Practical *confession* of sin and steadfast *growth* in the Word were seen in analogies drawn at the Dung and Fountain Gates.

But now, King Jesus wants to open a flowing stream of fresh, living water by the fulfilling of His promise to you: "You shall receive the gift of the Holy Spirit!"[7]

To His promise of salvation's "fountain of water springing up into everlasting life,"[8] Jesus adds the offer of His Spirit's "rivers of living water flowing from within you."[9]

Jesus wants you to be filled with the Holy Spirit. Here is a resource of power, flowing from an unending source. "Spirit fullness" can alleviate your thirst, strengthen you when you're under attack, provide refreshment through daily prayer and praise in the Spirit, and release a flow of Christ's healing power through you to others.

Ask Jesus to fill you with the Holy Spirit. Praisefully come into His presence and by faith receive His promise: "The promise is to you!"[10]

Expect His miraculous touch upon you as He answers your hunger and thirst.

After you have been filled, keep a fresh walk in Spirit-fullness. Ephesians 5:18 literally reads, "[Keep on being] filled with the Spirit." Don't only say, "I'll drink at the well." But having been satisfied, keep coming daily to the King's Pool. Keep the fountain flowing in your soul!

....

SPIRITUAL WORKOUT

1. What issues in your life tend to bring you to impatience, doubt or discouragement about there ever being improvement toward what you believe would please the Lord?

2. Have you experienced, or been witness to, an instantaneous healing such as that of the Hayfords' little boy's feet? (What is your reaction to the "ordinariness" of the way that phenomenal thing took place?)

3. What roadblocks to our personal growth can result from habitually expecting miracles to solve our problems? On the other hand, what dangers lie in not expecting or relying on the availability of God's miraculous intervention in our lives?

4. Discuss the relationship between God's Word and honest confession, as a means of living at "The Fountain Gate." How has both using and responding to the Word of God brought about progressive purification in your life?

5. *The Williams New Testament* translates 1 John 1:7, "But if we continue to live in the light, just as He is in the light...the blood of Jesus His Son continues to cleanse us from every sin." What encouraging promise and hope does this verse have for sins of which we are unaware?

6. Close this session with prayers that focus on any confession of unpurged sin anyone in the group would like to make—either privately or in open, humble acknowledgment of need—in the presence of the Lord.

CHAPTER TWELVE

Knowing How God Feels About You

The Word:

Nehemiah 2:16-20

And the officials did not know where I had gone or what I had done; I had not yet told the Jews, the priests, the nobles, the officials, or the others who did the work. Then I said to them, "You see the distress that we are in, how Jerusalem lies waste, and its gates are burned with fire. Come and let us build the wall of Jerusalem, that we may no longer be a reproach." And I told them of the hand of my God which had been good upon me, and also of the king's words that he had spoken to me. So they said, "Let us rise up and build." Then they set their hands to this good work.

But when Sanballat the Horonite, Tobiah the Ammonite official, and Geshem the Arab heard of it, they laughed at us and despised us, and said, "What is this thing that you are doing? Will you rebel against the king?" So I answered them, and said to them, "The God of heaven Himself will prosper us; therefore we His servants will arise and build, but you have no heritage or right or memorial in Jerusalem."

The Target:

- To understand how Almighty God feels about us as His sons, notwithstanding our weaknesses or clutter of problems.
- To see in Nehemiah's first conversation with the Jerusalemites, the loving spirit of the Holy Spirit.
- To recognize the difference between "feeling good about yourself" *within the circle of God's grace,* and feeling that way in *spite* of that grace.

KNOWING HOW GOD FEELS ABOUT YOU

There is something especially poignant about the mood of Nehemiah's first communication with the leaders of the Jewish community in Jerusalem. While they knew a visitor had arrived from Shushan, and they doubtless knew his respected office in Artaxerxes's court, Nehemiah himself relates to us that at this stage the officials did not know his reason for coming:

- They did not know his intent;
- They knew nothing of his midnight survey;
- They did not yet know the authority with which he came.

In fact, all the leaders knew, with the dawn of this conference's day, was that three days had passed since his arrival and he had called them to a meeting.

And they met.

And in this meeting with "the Jews, the priests, the nobles, the officials, or the others"[1] of the citizenry, the disclosure of the heart of a most unusual person takes place. The remarkable sensitivity and gentleness shown by Nehemiah has to have been much of the reason he elicited such trust and cooperation from the people. Hear his first words: "You see the distress that we are in...let us build...that we may no longer be a reproach."[2]

The magnanimity of this approach is in the manner with which Nehemiah completely identifies with the people: "You see the distress that *we* are in...let *us* build...that *we* may no longer be a reproach." Except for the nature and character of this man, we can readily create another scenario.

Imagine Nehemiah as having been so affected by his high court position that he comes to the people with something like this:

Ah...hem (self-importantly clearing his throat). I come

with greetings from the emperor's palace where, as I
believe you all are aware, I hold the position of cupbearer. (Dramatic pause, condescending smile.)

It is somewhat awkward for me to know how best to
say this. But, the fact is, I have come out of sheer frustration with the seemingly endless reports we receive in
Shushan. That is, reports that you, here, have somehow,
uh, not yet been able to get things in reasonable,
respectable order on your own.

(Now, with mild disdain.) Feeling concern as a Jew,
and with enough self-respect to disallow my being indif-
ferent, I have come to see something done about the
embarrassing state of affairs here. It is, really, don't you
think, inexcusable that the walls are still such a mess and,
of course, that the gates are in the same burned condition
as when Nebuchadnezzar left town 150 years ago?
Naturally I, and all of us Jews in Persia and elsewhere, are
disturbed. It's difficult for us to understand why something tangible can't have at least begun before now. After
all, what takes place here in Jerusalem reflects on all us
Jews wherever we are.

And so, (and I hope you can appreciate the sacrifice
and the inconvenience), I have made this trip to come
and provide some leadership, with orders from
Artaxerxes mandating your cooperation. Naturally, I'm
hoping I won't have to apply the power of my office. My
letters allow me considerable authority should I need it.
And I am concerned with your general and obvious lack
of motivation regarding the walls.

(Scanning the group with a twisted smile.) Presuming
this will change, I am hopeful of your recognizing that my
time is important and the opportunity and the benefit is
entirely yours. I don't need this work and I might well
have remained in Shushan. But in hopes that my patrio-
tism and good will toward you and the project will ignite
the best in you all, I am now ready to begin. I'll be issu-
ing orders later this week and will expect work teams to
be on time.

*I'm sure you can't help but be thankful that the days of
your ridiculous appearance in the eyes of neighboring
peoples are shortly to conclude. If I can get what I expect
out of you, I'll have this project sewed up in reasonably
short order and be able to get back to Persia.
Am I understood? (daDA—daDA—daDA!)*

This may sound and stage like cheap melodrama. It deserves to. But
the pretentious manner of such self-importance is not difficult to
envision—we've all seen that disgusting, patronizing spirit in someone
at sometime.

Yet Nehemiah is so completely opposite to this scenario that it is
not only refreshing, but it is also beautifully instructive. His way with
those he's come to help is marvelously characteristic of the way the
Bible reveals God's feelings toward us—and how He wants us to think
about ourselves.

FEELING GOOD ABOUT YOURSELF

We hear a great deal of talk today about "how you feel about yourself"—and with good reason. There are so many forces that reduce
one's sense of self-worth or self-esteem, and many of us can easily feel
unnecessary, unwanted and useless. Society's attempted answer for
countering this syndrome is usually to mount a self-help program—an
effort with either a physical, material or psychological base. Entire
cable television networks exist to show you how to feel better about
yourself through improving your physique, learning new skills, striking it rich with money schemes, releasing or rejuvenating your sex life,
creating the new you or learning to resolve negativism, inner tension
or psychological blocks. Everything is proposed from a new suit to a
new spouse, from a new job to a new hobby or from group therapy to
a master's degree.

As so often with us humans, we recognize need but tend to answer
it with temporary measures at best and with destructive ones at worst.

It is nice to feel good about yourself and I've counseled enough
people in my pastoral ministry to know how poor an image many people have of themselves. Even with the more secure among us, there is
enough negative or painful input in our backgrounds that virtually

none are without the need of affirmation, support and a general, periodic positive message to our egos.

I'm not talking cheap flattery or manipulative lingo.

People don't need flattery. They don't need crutches for their identities; they need permanent, healing reinforcement. But human

—▲—

"YOU HAVE MADE US FOR YOURSELF," AUGUSTINE

WROTE OF GOD, "AND OUR SOULS FIND NO REST

UNTIL THEY FIND IT IN YOU."

—▼—

resources, however sincerely motivated or professionally administered, can never effect a completely satisfying answer for the *whole* man.

As created beings, each person has an intuitive sense of responsibility to God. Try as he might, by whatever philosophical or scientific argument, man's effort at explaining away this accountability always fails to satisfy the depth of the real hunger. "You have made us for yourself," Augustine wrote of God, "and our souls find no rest until they find it in you." Still, many labor diligently, yet vainly, hoping to reestablish their own personhood and self-confidence without coming to terms with their relationship to and understanding of the One who made them.

Nehemiah's sensitive approach in beginning assistance to the people of Jerusalem is important for more than diplomatic reasons. Humanly speaking, he will obviously have a much better chance at strong work relations by treating the people with respect. But the deeper issue in his style is how clearly his words and behavior reveal a true, deep-seated sense of identity *with* those he has come to help.

Nehemiah is a man who surrendered high position at the world capital, endured an incredibly demanding trip, prepared extensively to supply a multiple-years-long project, arrived with the support of royal troops and still demanded nothing of honor or deference from the Jerusalem elders. Instead he personally, gently and graciously identifies with their plight. He becomes one with them.

You may have had experience in your career with a supervisor like that. You may even be a supervisor who sees the elegant effectiveness of this style of leadership. Chances are, however, that you've also seen the other kind of supervisor—the one whose own ego is so fragile that he can keep it intact only by tearing down his "inferiors."

The style of leadership we see in Nehemiah is more than humane, judicious and gentlemanly. It is divine. This is the way of the Almighty God in seeking to redeem man. It is the method of the Son of God in His incarnate approach to us all. And it is the manner of the Spirit of God as He comes to help, to heal, to strengthen and to rebuild the personalities of those Christ has redeemed.

For any thoughtful person, the most humbling fact revealed through the Bible is not our guilt before God because of our sin. Far more humbling is that the God who made us and whom we disobeyed has chosen to love us rather than damn us. An honest look at our muddle—whether personal or the entire human race—is sufficient to justify God's decision, should He simply say, "I'm tired of this tribe. Disintegrate the whole lot."

If God exists, no one should blame Him if He scratched out the planet, vaporized its inhabitants and started over in some clean corner of the galaxy. But instead, "God so loved the world that He gave His only begotten Son, that whoever believes in Him should not perish but have everlasting life. For God did not send His Son into the world to condemn the world, but that the world through Him might be saved."[3]

And this love expressed itself in a way that has come to meet us where we are: "And the Word became flesh and dwelt among us, and we beheld His glory, the glory as of the only begotten of the Father, full of grace and truth....No one has seen God at any time. The only begotten Son...has declared Him."[4]

The whole program of God's redemption is one of loving identification with its subjects—with us. And a real understanding response to this incredible reality will form the only true basis for anyone learning to feel good about himself. When it begins to dawn upon me that God not only loves and reaches *to* me, but is also unashamed to completely identify *with* me, I have discovered a foundation for recovering any lost sense of personal worth or self-esteem.

Nehemiah's words point out three things characterizing the Holy Spirit's mission to rebuild us:

- He is *compassionate* with us.
- He is *committed* to help us.
- He is *companioned* beside us.

Compassion: "Look at the distress we are in." The words flow with patience, are absent of criticism and pulsate with understanding. They seem to say, "Your distress is my distress. I don't see *you* as a problem, I see the problem as *ours*."

Commitment: "Let us rise up and build." The invitation is to partnership, not servitude. The heart of God is revealed as fully set on ennobling us, the fallen. His redemption is designed to restore our joint-heirship.[5]

Companionship: "That we no longer be a reproach." What? We a reproach? Nehemiah had nothing to be ashamed of, and neither has God. And still He comes to companion so completely with His beloved creature, man, that His Holy Spirit breathes to our hearts: "You were made in His image, and until it's restored, He considers your incompletion a reduction of His purpose. He will not rest until His character is vindicated by its fullest, most beautiful recovery in you."

Clearly God's desire is to restore *all* of you, as a person, and all of us, plural, as the Body of Christ. This is part of the grand and exciting potential of God's movement among men in our day. And as we move, personally and collectively, toward internalizing God's compassion, commitment and companionship, we'll find that His grounds for feeling better about ourselves far surpass mere psychological ones.

Let's look closely at Jesus, as He teaches about God's heart toward us: it's both strengthening and affirming.

THE SON, TEACHING US
ABOUT THE FATHER'S HEART

Luke's record of Jesus' life presents a trilogy of stories He told to answer critics. Religious leaders were constantly irritated with Jesus. His teaching raised their hackles time and again as He confronted their empty notions about God.

One of their most severe bones of contention was Christ's receptivity toward people whom the religionists rejected as unworthy. "Then all the tax collectors and the sinners drew near to hear Him. And the

Pharisees and scribes complained, saying, 'This man receives sinners.'"[6] Following this rumble, as though to add the last straw, Jesus had dinner with a group of the religious rejects.

A dramatic tension is present here.

On the one hand, the sinful with whom Jesus met represent a hidden hope in the soul of all of us who fail. Somehow we sense that the *real* God would not abandon us because of our need, but the *religious* God seems to turn away.

The Pharisees were the personification of the latter and certainly the same spirit prevails today. But into this milieu of mixed hope and

---

YOU'RE WORTH EVERYTHING TO HIM! YOUR FAILURES HAVE NOT REMOVED YOUR POSSIBILITIES!

---

uncertainty about God's real nature, Jesus steps forth. His words answer to the secret hopes we hold, and His candor silences the Pharisee within or outside us, who shouts, "You're beyond God's point of patience! He hasn't time for washouts." And so it was that Jesus taught three consecutive parables just to show us God's heart and to give us a clear picture of how God feels about you and me.

The first parable[7] is the lesson of the one lost sheep. Jesus tells of a shepherd concerned for *each* member of his flock. He pictures God's heart as searching for even one person missing from among a hundred. The message is on *worth*: None of us is less important to Him because we're but one among the multitudes of humanity.

In the second parable[8] Jesus describes a woman who had lost one of 10 coins. These were not ordinary coins, for in that culture they were the equivalent of an engagement ring in ours. To the woman they meant *promise*—they meant hope. The issue was more than value, it was *vision*—tomorrow's dream.

And so the woman zealously sweeps her house, looking for the lost coin—the uncompleted hope, so to speak. And upon finding it, she cries for joy, "Rejoice with me, I've found what I lost!"

In this account, Jesus helps us hear God's heart as saying, "I know you feel the desire for completeness, so *know this:* You're an unfulfilled promise on My side of the ledger, too. I'm as desirous of your completion as you are, and I have committed Myself to fulfill the dreams I've put in your heart. Since you want *Me* as I do *you,* be assured—we are going to rejoice together in finding and fulfilling your deepest longings."

The third parable, the story of the Prodigal Son, is one of Jesus' most magnificent (read Luke 15:11-32). Here is God's heart completely unveiled. He reaches out to the most unjustifiably rebellious and miserable failure. After reading that story of consummate waste and ruined potential, *now* ask the question: How does God—Father, Son and Holy Spirit—feel about me, my failures, my needs and my waste of divinely-provided opportunities?

Jesus' teaching gives an unmistakable answer: You're worth everything to Him! Your failures have not removed your possibilities! As Bill Gaither has so aptly said it, "The One who knows me best, loves me most!"

When this perception dominates, a completely different posture toward God can develop in us. When need rises or sin clouds your fellowship, your sense of acceptance remains firm. "Don't let go of your prospect of hope, for you do not have a High Priest untouched by your feelings of weakness. Rather, He understands your temptation, having been tempted as you are. But He remained sinless."[9]

RESOLVING A NECESSARY QUESTION

"Hey, wait!" someone feels constrained to inquire, "if God remained sinless, how can I come to Him?" That is a wise and needed question. We *should* care about sin's effect on His feelings. But the following verse gives His answer: "Come boldly to the throne of grace...and find grace to help in time of need."[10]

"But, Jack," someone schooled in theology might ask, "aren't you taking too light a view of sin? Doesn't it make *any* difference?"

To the contrary, I take a very stern view of sin. The Bible is very pointed on that subject: Sin can never be regarded lightly. To be emphatic and totally scriptural, it was *my* sin and *your* sin that is as responsible for killing Jesus as anyone else's. I am equally responsible with all who shouted for His crucifixion, and so are you. Our deeds—your sin and mine—made the sacrifice of Christ's life necessary. So the answer is: Yes. Sin has made a great difference! We *are* dealing with a holy God. And yet, all that notwithstanding, He has made it wonderfully clear that we are in His heart and on His mind.

> Jesus completely understands you
>   because of what
>   He went through as a man.
>   Jesus understands completely
>   because He was tempted
>   at every point that you are.

And, hallelujah! This Sinless One says, "Come boldly to my throne and find grace!" This isn't a call to reckless offense on our part. It isn't a brash boldness, but a confident certainty. The word for boldness here—*paresis*—reflects an open-faced, head-upraised ability to come with a full sense of acceptance. And such a posture does not result from a light view of sin. It is the fruit of understanding that *all* Jesus did on the cross is *so* complete, and its victory is *so* verified by His resurrection, that God calls us to never wallow in guilt, rejection or hopelessness. We are to come directly to His Throne!

Nehemiah said then, "I told them of the hand of my God which had been good upon me, and also of the king's words that he had spoken to me."[11] In the same way the Holy Spirit wants to assure you now. God's "good hand"—His pleasure to receive and to work with our need—is upon you.

STANDING IN FULL CONFIDENCE

And so it was the people who took heart at Nehemiah's words and said, "'Let us rise up and build,' [and] they set their hands to do this good work."[12]

But just as soon as they did, they were immediately beset by opponents: "But when Sanballat the Horonite, Tobiah the Ammonite official, and Geshem the Arab heard of it, they laughed at us and despised us, and said, 'What is this thing that you are doing? Will you rebel against the king?'"[13]

This mocking confrontation portrays the predictable method of satanic opposition. It is always hurled at you just when hope has begun to rise. As soon as faith comes—"God is *really* going to work something beautiful in my life"—and as soon as you respond with a will to partner with His Spirit, you can count on it: Sanballat—the accuser, Satan—will scream, "You have no right to even *think* of that! Are you about to rebel against the king?"

This translates to his classic "intimidation-in-the-name-of-godliness" tactic: "Wait!" he shrills. "Don't you realize your past life has removed your right to future fulfillment? You've rebelled against God's holy standards and now you think you deserve His blessing? You're dreaming!"

But the Holy Spirit will stand by you, just as Nehemiah arose, to declare to Sanballat, "The God of heaven Himself will prosper us; therefore we His servants will arise and build."[14]

That's the reason for God's assurance that He will prosper our efforts and restore our lives. *He is for us!* "And if God be for us, who be against us? Who has the right to condemn us?"[15]

Nehemiah crushes Sanballat's case with the words, "You have no heritage, or right or memorial in Jerusalem."[16] In curt words spoken with regal authority, the adversary's last claim is removed. And let it be so with you. Receive the Comforter's declaration, and rejoice in this knowledge:

- You now belong to the Lord your Savior, Almighty!
- He is totally committed to your fulfillment!
- He has willed the completion of His created purpose in your life!

Say, "Amen!!"

....

SPIRITUAL WORKOUT

1. Describe a boss or supervisor you've known who, like Nehemiah, was able to identify with workers and lead by becoming one with them instead of "lording it over" his "underlings."

2. Has your exposure to Christianity been a positive or a neg-

ative factor in your self-esteem? What pitfalls in both directions should Christians avoid?

3. Read Genesis 1:27. What bearing should this truth have on how we feel about ourselves?

4. How do parents often exert (a) positive and (b) negative influence on their children's self-concepts? Did you bring a positive or a negative self-concept from your own childhood?

5. Do you somehow sense that Jesus identifies with your weaknesses more readily than God the Father? Why or why not?

6. Identify any "Sanballats" in your circumstance or whom you have observed, who are inclined to tear down or belittle individuals or groups of believers.

PART THREE

SUSTAINING THE CITADEL

Jerusalem's walls shine in the sun,
Her glory now restored.
Her radiance a sign to all,
Her gates shout, "Praise the Lord!"

And I my hallelujahs join;
I too am made complete.
And in the Light of lights I'll walk,
Until in heav'n I meet
the One Who saved me.

—J.W.H.

Map of City and Diagram of Person

This simple map of Jerusalem shows the walls
as finished during Nehemiah's time.

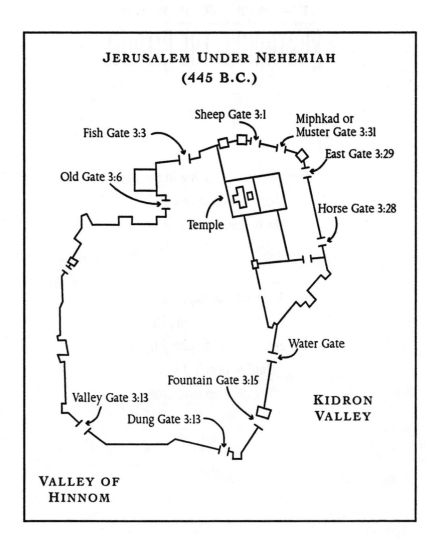

JERUSALEM UNDER NEHEMIAH
(445 B.C.)

Sheep Gate 3:1

Miphkad or
Muster Gate 3:31

Fish Gate 3:3

East Gate 3:29

Old Gate 3:6

Horse Gate 3:28

Temple

Water Gate

Fountain Gate 3:15

KIDRON
VALLEY

Valley Gate 3:13

Dung Gate 3:13

VALLEY OF
HINNOM

CHAPTER THIRTEEN

People Who Need People

The Word:

Nehemiah 3:1-4,6,12-15,26,28,29,31,32

Then Eliashib the high priest rose up with his brethren the priests and built the Sheep Gate; they consecrated it and hung its doors. They built as far as the Tower of the Hundred, and consecrated it, then as far as the Tower of Hananel. Next to Eliashib the men of Jericho built. And next to them Zaccur....Also the sons of Hassenaah built the Fish Gate; they laid its beams and hung its doors with its bolts and bars. And next to them Meremoth....Moreover Jehoiada...repaired the Old Gate....And next to him was Shallum the son of Hallohesh, leader of half the district of Jerusalem; he and his daughters made repairs. Hanun and the inhabitants of Zanoah repaired the Valley Gate....Malchijah...repaired the Refuse Gate; he built it and hung its doors with its bolts and bars. Shallun...leader of the district of Mizpah, repaired the Fountain Gate....Moreover the Nethinim who dwelt in Ophel made repairs...of the Water Gate....Beyond the Horse Gate the priests made repairs....After them Zadok...made repairs in front of his own house. After him Shemaiah the son of Shechaniah, the keeper of the East Gate, made repairs....After him Malchijah, one of the goldsmiths, made repairs as far as the house of the Nethinim and of the merchants, in front of the Miphkad Gate, and as far as the upper room at the corner. And between the upper room at the corner, as far as the Sheep Gate, the goldsmiths and the merchants made repairs.

The Target:

- To see the importance God puts on each individual, and the purposes He advances by involving us with one another.
- To confront individualistic resistance or fear of growing in and building mutually trusting relationships with others in Christ.
- To understand the meaning of the biblical idea of *submission*, and to come to terms with its application to our lives in order that we might be *built up* as well as help in *building others.*

People Who Need People

Name lists. Old-fashioned, hard-to-pronounce name lists. They constitute whole chapters of the Bible and make for tough, if not boring, reading. Nehemiah 3 is the first of such chapters in this book. I was about to skip it, thinking our study purposes could do without it, until I was reminded of a lesson I learned long ago.

One day I was struggling through the first chapter of Matthew—another name list—and began thinking, *What a strange way to begin the New Testament.* But I paused to inquire of the Lord, asking Him to teach me the answer to my question. As I prayed, the Holy Spirit helped me to see at least three reasons God put name lists in His Word:

1. He cares about and remembers *people*, individually and by name.
2. He makes promises to *people* and keeps them.
3. He accomplishes His purpose in *people* and does it through *people*.

So it isn't a matter of belaboring this chapter in order to wring something clever from it. Its very existence sounds forth *three* truths even before we begin! But yet another truth is of enormous value in deepening our understanding of the rebuilding process...

WE REALLY NEED EACH OTHER

This chapter describes the organization of the grand, sweeping reconstruction project of the walls. Even though the perimeter was more than two miles around, the following is a complete description of how it progressed.

Each specific section of the wall and each of the 10 gate sites were assigned to large family groups or to the members of smaller villages that surrounded Jerusalem. They were formed into teams under

Nehemiah's direction, and upon closer inspection, what at first appears to be a tedious recitation of names begins to throb with life and truth.

The facts: Thirty-eight different leaders are listed, men from at least eight different vocational callings. Seven villages provided volunteers, seven different rulers lead community groups and numerous family

---

OUR VERTICAL GROWTH IN CHRIST CANNOT BE
DISSOCIATED FROM OUR HORIZONTAL GROWTH
WITH PEOPLE AROUND US.

---

relationships are cited—even a man and his daughters. Clearly all vocations and a full spectrum of age groups are involved. What do the facts reveal? *The only way the wall was rebuilt was by people allowing other people to help alongside them!*

"Not too original," you might say. And I agree. But an obvious, oft-repeated truth, frequently disregarded because it lacks flair, is usually "oft repeated" with good reason. It holds a practical wisdom—it works.

The heart of this text holds a call to open up to other people, though it's something most of us fear or resist. As in ancient Jerusalem, we are each surrounded by others in whom God is working His plan. They're around me—and you, too. He calls us both to responsibly, honestly and receptively respond to His purpose in our teamwork. In the process of rebuilding, we will find that our progress *upward* is proportionate to our openness *outward*. Our vertical growth in Christ cannot be dissociated from our horizontal growth with people around us.

I need to remember that I'm not the only person God is rebuilding right now. As in Nehemiah's day, when the whole wall was going up at once, a massive recovery project is taking place everywhere. The Holy Spirit is not only restoring the whole *you*, He is also seeking to renew the whole Church! The implications of that fact are very real at a personal level, for the bottom line of this text's lesson underscores how very much we all really do need each other.

The principal group with whom you and I are involved is family—our brothers and sisters in Christ—and they parallel the Jerusalem wall-building team. I hope you have been a part of some of the marvelous gatherings of men in our time that emphasize this truth. God is showing thousands of men the need to relate to their wives and their children, to their brothers and sisters in Christ, to their pastors, to their congregations—all as men ready to accept their responsibilities as spiritual leaders—as dynamic builders of relationships.

One of the very saddest of all counseling opportunities a minister can have is helping a middle-aged man deal with the emotional walls his children have erected to keep him out of their lives because he was not emotionally present for them as younger children. When they needed him in their most formative years, he was building a career instead of a home. Now that they are approaching young adulthood, he wants desperately to be a part of such momentous decisions as choosing a mate. Too often, however, it is too late—not too late, of course, for the Spirit's balm to heal such wounds, but too late for the necessary bridges to be built.

And beyond this, we all need to learn to interrelate as members of Christ's Body. There are those around you experiencing the Holy Spirit's help toward their completeness, maturity and wholeness in the same way He is helping you. For some things to get done in you, you have to recognize your brothers and sisters in Jesus. We cannot see our lives completed by ourselves. The Holy Spirit is our primary Helper, but He has willed to use us all as instruments in each other's lives.

I need you to help complete what I'm to become. And you need me and the several others who touch your life. The contacts come through domestic, business, community, educational and spiritual relationships. Not everyone contributes in the same way, and at times some may seem more a liability than an asset to your building program. But the Word of God reminds us, "For none of us lives to himself, and no one dies to himself."[1]

That one verse summarizes a biblical principle that is far more than a mere social commentary recommending mutual goodwill. It is a conclusive statement from the Holy Spirit teaching us that our lives are irrevocably integrated in the affairs of others. If you try to avoid learning what God wants to do through those relationships, you withdraw at your own expense. You'll be poorer for having done so. In short, God is telling us we need to learn to live together. Growth and healing require us to learn interdependency, and we can only gain by learning to do so.

COMING TO A COMMITMENT

Do you find it difficult to relate to people, to open up and to break out? Practical problems do hinder some, especially those of us who limit our fellowshipping with our brothers and sisters in Christ as we need to do.

For example, have you felt hesitant to reach out? I often have. And I've been helped in learning to discover causes for my reluctance.

Some of us fear entering relationships or becoming too dependent on them because a past association ended in disappointment and failure. Many have entered a trusting relationship only to be left with the debris of broken trust and with draining wounds to their souls. To overcome the remembered pain of such experiences and to avoid being hindered in our futures, we need to hear the Spirit's call to a new starting point.

The mutual interdependence of Nehemiah's host of workers points to that beginning place—to crowd out fear or reluctance through the "lovelight" of God's Word on this subject. Love can cast out fear and truth will set free.[2] The truth about interrelationships, as a part of God's "wholeness program," can loose any tangle of emotions or memories that can obstruct your realizing the you God has intended.

We need to be freed from fears that hinder our coming to a commitment, because our sustaining a strong life in Christ once the walls are rebuilt greatly depends on our relationships with others. The recovery is only the beginning; the continuance is the objective. We need each other as much beyond the rebuilding project as we do during it.

SUBMITTING TO ONE ANOTHER

To shed the light of Scripture on the Bible pathway to relationships, one key subject must be discussed. Because it is so essential, it is not surprising that both flesh and devil conspire to keep it misunderstood.

Too often have fleshly, control-oriented people, jealous of power, taken the idea of submission to apply to everyone but themselves. Not only does that discourage some from opening to understand and practice "submission," but the devil has also been at work in some media reports about the men's movement.

Unwarranted claims are made by secularized opponents, shouting their opinion that the men's movement is promoting the notion that men are to assume a dominating role over their wives. This is, of course, not only a lie—but it negates the Holy Spirit's work among men who are answering His call to become true *servants* to their families. Servanthood is what true "submission" is about.

So examine with me the biblical idea of submission. In the last analysis, a right understanding and response to this concept is the God-given springboard to advance and grow in healthy, fulfilling relationships.

To begin, the Bible says that all believers are to "Submit to one another in the fear of God."[3] "Yes, all of you be submissive to one another, and be clothed with humility."[4] Note that this last passage follows Peter's affirmation that slaves should be in submission to their masters, wives to their husbands and young people to older people. These are role relationships, not superior-inferior designations. Lest any of these "submissive" relations be seen in that latter erroneous light, Peter adds the universal touch: Everyone is to have a submissive attitude toward everyone else.

These direct commands teach that (a) our submission is an evidence of our respect and reverence for God's purpose; and (b) we are to do so with a gracious attitude toward other persons in Christ's Body.

Notice that the circle of our call to mutual submission is within the fellowship of faith. The Bible doesn't direct us to randomly submit to anybody. It calls for this spirit of growth and trust within the community of the redeemed; a growth in relationships and healing among those who have been forgiven and who honestly want to grow forward in Christ's purpose for them.

But what does "submit" mean? Is it a call to some mechanical program of depersonalization or to some reduction of my personality? Is it a denial of my own decision-making powers or a placing of my destiny at the mercy or the whim of others?

Those questions arise because for many, the word "submission" has become synonymous with self-abnegation—with a "doormat" mentality. To submit to somebody, they suppose, requires that they grant a license for anyone who wishes to "walk all over me." Any sensible person's reaction to such a proposition automatically closes the subject. Therefore submission is out—the victim of gross misdefinition and

---

A TRUE UNDERSTANDING OF SUBMISSION IS IN

SEEING ITS VOLUNTARY NATURE—A CHOICE TO

TRUST AND A CHOICE TO LOVE.

---

misunderstanding. Moreover, human rights and personal freedom are the catchwords of our culture and submission sounds too much like a denial of rights.

But what is *really* meant by the word "submission"?

Although I agree that some exaggerated teaching and exploitive applications of authority have equated submission with authoritarianism or exploitation, needless to say, this was never God's intent for us or the meaning as it occurs in His Word. Let's take a fresh look in the Bible. For if resistance is due to misunderstanding, then understanding may result in responsiveness. And the importance is crucial, because if we reject the key to learning about the real meaning of submissive relationships, we may miss God's key to our growth.

The call to "submit to one another" is easier to answer with peaceful confidence when a proper definition is known. Submission is translated from the Greek word *hupotasso*, and is derived from the prefixed preposition *hupo* and the verb *tasso*. Technically its etymology renders the meaning, "to place under." But the actual verbal meaning is not that severe.

First, submission in its truest sense can only be given; it cannot be exacted. A demanded submission, one that is surrendered against the fullhearted consent of the one "submitting," is not truly submissive.

Forced submission is actually subjugation—the mastery of one party by another. The heart isn't in it. The beginning of a true understanding of submission is in seeing its voluntary nature—a choice to trust and a choice to love.

Further truth exudes from this verb when we trace its historical usage. In the Greek culture, the fundamental idea of *hupotasso* related to fixed positions of authority and subordinancy. It was a basic military term describing the right arrangement of troops for structuring people in strategic relationship; so arranged for the purpose of insuring their mutual protection and their collective arrival at victory.

Years ago I learned something of this meaning of submission and it was through experiencing this very setting. I was part of a reserve military training program. During my training, I was taught how a small team of soldiers—a squad—were to move forward in enemy territory. Each man had an assigned place in formation following the lead soldier. Each was to proceed in a way that so related our positions to each other that we "covered" one another. Each soldier was responsible for perceiving his role as designed to maximize the safety and security of the others in his squad, platoon or company.

That military meaning is the essence of the New Testament idea of submission in relationships. It holds nothing of reducing one another, but everything of protecting each other; with being sensitive to one another; with being sensible and serving in our relationships with one another. It includes accountability and is not without mutual acknowledgment of appropriate authority. There are no *doormats*—only brothers and sisters, sons and daughters of the Father.

The Bible speaks a great deal of this kind of life-to-life relationship with one another: "We, being many, are one body in Christ, and individually members of one another."[5]

Being "joined and knit together by what every joint supplies... [which] causes growth of the body for the edifying of itself in love."[6] That is *hupotasso!*—the kind of submission we are called to in Christ's Body.

PARTNERING WITH THE BODY OF CHRIST

This was the original New Testament idea in "joining" a church; it was, and can be today, a knitting of lives together in a supportive, healing fellowship. You and I must consider coming to a point where we acknowledge that the completion of our growth is going to have to involve other brothers and sisters in Christ. In restoring the human personality, I come to terms with the fact that just as Jerusalem's wall would never have been completed without each Jew partnering with the rest, so *I* am only going to be put together through interrelationships with other members of the Body of Christ. As Nehemiah led these ancient Jews in a rebuilding partnership, the Holy Spirit wants to lead us in relationships with one another.

We need to open up to real mutual dependence upon one another. That is what healthy congregations are about. That's why the holy dynamic of small group fellowship is being rediscovered today, for in such settings the love of God flows healing to the members of Christ's Body.

And in that life flow, yet another mighty thing will occur. Jesus said, "When you love one another, the world is going to believe."[7] He assured us in advance what has been proven again and again. As outsiders see the love shown and the mutual blessing realized by Christians who grow *together*, they say, "I would love to be a part of that kind of thing. These people really care about each other." The net result of wholeness in the Body is evangelism of the lost. Submission is neither an isolated activity of people who surrender personhood, nor an exercise in religious piety. It is dynamic, as was the progress on the building of Jerusalem's walls.

Time and again we read in Nehemiah 3, "After him"..."next to him." People were involved together in the repair and rebuilding process, and everyone around could see the fruit of their union.

Today, those who stand with us in Christ are part of God's program for helping us get the job done. We need them, but they need us too. Our submission to one another makes the way for a great building process to be accomplished. If you are not yet in a community of believers, join with a group of brothers and sisters who *are* committed to growing in Christ as a caring group.

Perhaps you are one who has resisted this need for growth in relationships because of having been hurt by people in the Church. Don't avoid this because of past hurts. Unfortunately some have been wounded in Church relationships; or maybe just didn't like the way they were treated. Perhaps you or someone you know was even sorely misunderstood or cruelly violated. But it wasn't the "relationship" that didn't work; it was *people* who didn't function in the Spirit of

Christ! Those are disappointing experiences, but they shouldn't sour anyone on "the Church."

And moreover, make no mistake: *You* and *I* have sometimes been "those people" who hurt others. We must honestly admit that we can

---

THE ANSWER TO A SAD HISTORY IS NOT FUTURE ISOLATION.

---

all be so blind to our own personal shortcomings that we have probably failed at times to see how we ourselves contributed to some relational disappointments.

Innocent people have often suffered great wrong at the hands of Christian institutions—even excommunication without consideration. But the answer to a sad history is not future isolation. Someone said years ago, "There are no Lone Rangers in the kingdom of God. Even the Lone Ranger needed Tonto." The need and the scriptural call to healing fellowship is clear.

So, acknowledge your membership. Be part of a church family and receive the healing and the therapy that comes to the personality through this God-ordained way. Say, "I am a part of this Body," and acknowledge it to the eldership or pastoral leadership in that assembly. Such open declaration is the biblical pattern of submitting to and receiving one another. It's saying, "This place is where I company. I'm not just a religious roustabout. I'm a person who, as in Nehemiah, is next to...who is next to...who is next to...." And together we will be built up as a spiritual house in Christ.[8]

....

SPIRITUAL WORKOUT

1. Do you feel that it's more difficult for men to make close friends than for women? Is it harder for older people than younger?

2. Have you had an experience, within the Church or without, that made it hard for you to reach out to others?

3. If you are married, how do you and your spouse work out Peter's admonition for wives to be in submission to their husbands (see 1 Pet. 3:1)?

4. What abuses must be avoided in carrying out the principle that children are to be in submission to their parents?

5. What "Lone Ranger" attitudes can hinder genuine, intimate fellowship among God's people?

6. How is leadership supposed to work in a church that takes seriously the principle of everyone being in submission to each other?

CHAPTER FOURTEEN

HELL'S ANTIHOPE PROGRAM

The Word:

Nehemiah 4:1,2

But it so happened, when Sanballat heard that we were rebuilding the wall, that he was furious and very indignant, and mocked the Jews. And he spoke before his brethren and the army of Samaria, and said, "What are these feeble Jews doing? Will they fortify themselves? Will they offer sacrifices? Will they complete it in a day? Will they revive the stones from the heaps of rubbish—stones that are burned?"

The Target:

- To examine our idea of what our Adversary, the devil, is really like in order to have a clear, biblical and mature view of his total commitment to oppose us in any way possible.
- To see in Sanballat and his companions a parallel picture of some of the tactics the Enemy attempts to work toward discouragement, mockery and defeat.
- To be reminded that the rubble of our pasts is not only destined for God's gracious removal and recovery, but that He is even able to use the broken parts of our pasts as contributive to His purposes in building His purpose in us by His Spirit.

Hell's Antihope Program

We have learned that the devil is far more dangerous than the "sly old fox" the Sunday School chorus depicts. Neither is he a red-outfitted masquerade monster, replete with horns, pointed tail and a Neptunelike spear. Far more scripturally, Satan is the sinister embodiment of everything hateful; the sum of all that is heinous and hellish, and the chief spirit manipulating the violence of evil men and the viciousness of deadly disease.

To understand what Satan is like, look at the emaciated body of an African child in a nation ravaged by famine. Or, see bodies blown to pieces by a terrorist bomb.

That's satanic. That's what hell is up to.

Such scenes are not merely man at the mercy of the elements or man victimized by human viciousness. Such strife, suffering and bloodshed are motivated and mobilized by the spirit of hell. Jesus said so: "The thief comes to steal, to kill and to destroy."[1]

Look at a body racked by cancer, shriveled to virtual nonexistence except for slight palpitations of heartbeat. That's hell at work. Look at hearts broken in the wake of splintered homes. That's hell doing its best—at its worst. And when the newscasters report insanely brutal murders or embryos left in garbage sacks, that's hell.

But it is *no less* hell at work when you meet people who have lost hope, been reduced to despair or who become so futile about the future that they take their lives.

Have you seen hell at work "at work"? A man makes the "mistake" of saying an affirming word about a person one of the bosses dislikes— and the man is forever eliminated when promotions are in order. A woman comes down with a life-threatening illness, and management manages to find another reason to dismiss her when she knows in her heart it's because her condition would damage the company's self-insurance program. A worker makes a single mistake and is branded as a "loser." Such experiences can carry a weight of discouragement that can be lifted only by supernatural means—by Nehemiah's God—the God of hope.

The same "hell" is at work against you, personally, too.

When you study the grotesque signs of man's sin-drunken fall—

- deformed bodies;
- ruined minds;
- perverted values; and
- poisoned attitudes

—these are *all* the result of the impact of sin on our race. They are what Satan—and sin and death and hell—are all about, and it is your wisdom to recognize that same malevolence would like to crush you—and me.

Every single one of us has been, in one way or another, burned by hellfire. It's left its brand on us all. But Jesus Christ has come to wipe that away—literally, to "*cross* it out." By the power of Calvary He forgives and saves, and then He proceeds to rebuild and redirect the potential of our lives and fulfilling of our destinies. While the thief comes to destroy, Jesus says, "I have come that they may have life, and that they may have it more abundantly."[2]

We have discussed how the Holy Spirit brings about Christ's abundant life. Yet many become weary before hell's relentless tactics. Their destinies are in heaven, but they haven't seen "hell" vanquished in its continued assault on their personalities.

Even though Satan knows his authority over you was broken with Christ's entry into your life, that won't stop his efforts. He will consistently try to hinder God's program for you. Wherever physical, mental, emotional or other personal needs remain, he will seek to remove hopes and weaken your confidence in eventual completeness. This tactic at obstructing the Holy Spirit's work will succeed, unless you recognize his strategy and learn to resist him.[3]

In the person of Sanballat, we see in Nehemiah chapter 4 the satanic style of opposition we can expect after the Holy Spirit begins His work in us. As the enemy of Nehemiah's work with the Jews, Sanballat's words personify Satan's attempts at thwarting *us*.

Earlier, the building effort having recently begun, Sanballat laughed in open disdain at the Jews, seeking by mockery to discourage them and break their morale. But now the situation intensifies: "He was furious and very indignant...."[4] His mockery continued (for our Adversary will always seek to demean) and Sanballat's fury is boiling now. With the processes of time he sees his hold weakening and his capacity for successful resistance disappearing.

How closely this increased hatefulness parallels the Bible prophecies concerning satanic activity in our times. Revelation says, "The devil has come down with great fury, knowing he has but a short time."[5] Daniel describes the efforts of hell in the last days as bent on "wearing out" those who serve God.[6] This is not only something we all experience personally, it is increasingly observable everywhere around us.

You need not have lived very long to have perspective on the fact that in just the last few years a marked intensification of evil is manifest. Youth who have grown up during these recent years may suppose this is the way things have always been. But not so.

Even in the reasonably short life span of someone in their 40s, it is possible to measure the advancing intensity of the works of darkness. From the post-World War II years into and through the '60s and '70s (and as we now move toward the dawn of a new century), an awesome amplifying of sin and Satan's fury is in evidence. So many things, destructive to human hope, are scaling upward as reports tabulate increased crime, violence, suicide, divorce, mental illness, alcoholism, drug addiction and numberless other expressions of human failure. And with each device hell fabricates, another dimension of bondage associated with it comes to the surface. The problem is not merely the agony in each personal or social disaster, but the compounding effect they all have in the damage they leave behind. This can be multiplied well beyond the immediate individual involved.

- A suicide scars everyone associated.
- A divorce leaves the emotions of an entire family in shambles.
- A bankruptcy leaves the shame of embarrassment and guilt.
- A disease creates relational and psychological rubble.

All these situations leave remains in the lives of people touched by the failures of others, long after the initial pain is past or the principal party gone. These things are happening because of that forewarned word: "Satan has come down with great fury for he knows he has only a short time."[7]

These are the latter days. But I am persuaded that irrespective of how bleak the circumstances may seem or how shadowed the horizons may appear by reason of the Adversary's desperate and despicable tactics, Jesus has bequeathed to us a life of power and of triumph in the resources of His Kingdom. His Holy Spirit is still here to help us realize it! Perspective on the Adversary's tactics is always helpful to avoid being battered and bruised by blind-side assaults. The Lord Jesus has not called us to futility but to victory, and we *can* learn the path to His dominion over the devil. We *can* experience full deliverance and joy in believing.

Hallelujah! That's His way for us!

RELENTLESS ATTACK

Sanballat's indignant uprising is typical of our Adversary's continuing purpose. Settle your mind on this, saints: Satan never has a "good" day. Some people apparently labor under the illusion that the devil may occasionally relax his attack, as though he might rise on a Wednesday morning and say, "I think I'll go easy on 'em today." But forget it. Such

DON'T LET THE DEVIL REMIND YOU OF *YOUR*
WEAKNESS WHEN HIS *REAL* CONCERN IS HIS
LOSS OF POWER OVER YOU!

will never be the case. Our Adversary, the thief, comes *only* as Jesus said; to steal and to kill and to destroy. That's his entire program. Wrath, great indignation, mocking—it's the Sanballat syndrome—the picture of the devil.

Then Sanballat rose to speak before his brethren, the army of Samaria. (If you'll allow it, let's simply consider the "army of Samaria" as "demons—the hosts of hell.") In his address, Sanballat makes five statements, each one of which conveys a concept that can instruct us in the methods Satan uses to attack and remove hope.

"What are these feeble Jews doing?" His mocking statement is not directed to the Jews, for Sanballat is pep talking his troops. His first observation relates to the tactical vulnerability of "these feeble Jews."

What Sanballat is really doing is lamenting the fact that until now he has had complete control. As long as the Jews had no defenses, he could dominate them at will. While he was the governor of the entire region, and until Nehemiah's authority preempted his, Sanballat's rule was unchallenged. But now his only point of comfort is that his former subjects are still weakened, though their situation is fast changing.

Lesson: Don't let the devil remind you of *your* weakness when his *real* concern is his loss of power over you! The Spirit of God has come to dwell in you, and "He who is in you is greater than he who is in the world."[8] Silence the snide attack of Satan with your own declaration: "I may be weak in myself, but I don't stand alone." You'll discover as Paul did when he was under satanic attack, "When I am weak, then I am strong." Whatever weakness still remains, Jesus speaks the comforting words, "My grace is sufficient for you. My strength is made perfect in your weakness."[9]

HE ATTACKS YOUR FRAILTIES

Next, Sanballat asked, "Will they fortify themselves?" Later he will raise question as to Nehemiah's motivation, suggesting the rebuilding of the walls is a latent conspiracy against Artaxerxes. In truth, Sanballat could care less how the king felt. His concern was the loss of his own control, and he wanted the people with Nehemiah to think he had the king's interests at heart.

Have you ever noticed how amazingly noble Satan can suddenly become when he wants to intimidate a person? He'll say, "Be careful. Don't you see your *real* reason for trying to rebuild your life? You're just trying to gain independence—you're going to lose real humility. When you get it all together, do you know what's going to happen? You're going to stop trusting God. You would be much better off in need—better for you to remain in a defeated, enfeebled condition."

Some oft-employed devices along this line of hellish reasoning include:

- God somehow wants you sick because you'll trust Him more when you are unwell.
- It's the will of God that you have financial difficulty. It keeps you humble and dependent.
- It's the will of God for your business affairs to be under stress; it develops your character.
- It's God's will that you not advance beyond your present position at work. Water settles at its natural level, and you've reached yours.

I've even heard,

- It's God's will for me to divorce my wife, because she won't "agree" with me when I try to point out the answer to our problems, and the Bible says, "How can two walk together unless they are in agreement"!

But hell's lies need to be stuffed back down the Snake's throat, even though a relative truth is present when we note how pressure does drive us to faith and growth in character. Still, the absolute truth is more significant: God wants and wills to take you *through* to victory, to be able to say, "I can do all things through Christ who strengthens me."[10] Make no mistake—the devil isn't interested in your weakness for godly reasons. He wants to exploit your weakness, but the Holy Spirit has come to build you to a place of complete strength.

Sanballat's comment, "they'll fortify and rebel," is only reflective of Satan's concern with his lost dominion. It also indicates the incredible lengths to which He will go to create doubt that it is God's will for you to be fully restored.

HE ATTACKS YOUR WORSHIP OF GOD

Sanballat's third question to his troops accentuates the devil's demeaning, browbeating technique: "Will they offer sacrifices?"

On the subject of sacrifices, Sanballat knows from history that when this people worship their Lord, real power is generated! The implication of Sanballat's taunt is not regarding the location of their place of worship, for we know the Temple was finished and functional. His words focus instead on their walk and their witness. As long as the walls of the city are still in rubble, the liberty of the people in coming and going to worship was always threatened, for it was an unprotected city. Further, their vulnerability to mocking critics was still present: "Some God! Some city!"

Has anyone ever said to you, "And you call yourself a Christian!"? The obvious point of such a remark is that your deficiencies—being short of perfection—should prompt your withdrawal from claiming to be committed to Christ.

And our points of weakness can be terribly embarrassing!

How often have you felt compelled to concede your right to claim Jesus' name—to withdraw from worshiping Him with freedom and confidence? Many of us whom the Lord is wanting to bring into wholeness, stability and maturity have suffered this sense of shame, and Satan loves to capitalize on that.

This is the satanic spirit in Sanballat's question, "Will they offer sacrifices?" Have you heard Satan say such things to you? "Who do you think you are? Christian? What nerve to openly, declaratively and publicly worship your God when your life still shows signs of the past! You'll *never* qualify as a *real* worshiper!"

But listen, dear friend. Silence that liar with this truth: "My approach to God in public or private will yet be bold, for I have free access to Him through my Lord, Jesus Christ. It is Him I praise and through Him I worship. Be gone, you foul spirit!"

Our answer: "Yes! We *will* worship!"

SLOWNESS OF YOUR PROGRESS

In the fourth challenge, "Will they complete it in a day?" Sanballat insinuated that they would never get it done. It's the same kind of mockery that whispers to you, "You know, you can talk all you want, but you've attempted this before and thought about this for a long time, and it won't happen now, either."

From the text, we are given no idea how long this wall-rebuilding project might have been on the drawing board: probably long before Nehemiah's visit. We do know the Temple had been completed about 70 years earlier, and there is every reason to believe that plans for rebuilding the wall had existed before this. But the vast difference in the past *plans* and the present *pursuit* was Nehemiah!

Yet even with his help the progress is slow, and we will later sense the deep tiredness of people facing a seemingly endless process as they intone wearily, "There is so much rubbish."[11] Your Adversary will seek to work a soul-wearying loss of tenacity in your faith. When things seem to drag on and on, he'll chortle at you, "In a day? Ha!" But don't

---

GOD IS ABLE TO SO COMPLETELY REDEEM

AND RESTORE THAT HE CAN GLORIFY HIMSELF

IN THE MIDST OF AND OUT OF THE PIECES OF

YOUR BROKEN PAST!

---

forget the *whole* story! Times are different now, for your "Nehemiah" has come. If you listen to Him (when you don't see quick progress), when the enemy plays on that problem, the Comforter has the answer: "Let us not grow weary while doing good, for in due season we shall reap if we do not lose heart."[12]

His promise is certain. The completion may not be today, but the promise is God's guarantee! Take it, move forward toward tomorrow and don't hesitate in shouting the words in the face of hell: "I will reap victory's harvest because I'm *not* stopping now!"

HE RIDICULES YOUR BUILDING MATERIALS

Finally, Sanballat spouts, "Will they revive the stones from the heaps of rubbish—stones that are burned?"[13]

If you recall, when Nehemiah arrived the only materials he brought for the rebuilding program was timber. Thus, and logically, you might ask, "Where will they get the materials for the walls?" The answer is reasonable and thrilling in its significance: The walls will be completed by reclaiming, retooling, restoring and recovering the stones that comprise the rubbled mess!

What a message of hope that picture contains, and its truth applies to you. God is able to so completely redeem and restore that He can glorify Himself in the midst of and out of the pieces of your broken past! He is willing to remove the pain of your past and draw broken pieces back together: "The Spirit of the Lord is upon Me...to bind up the brokenhearted."[*] The same Holy Spirit is prepared to rebuild your new life and raise it up in splendor. It's true! How often have you heard people testify of the Lord taking the rubble of their failure and building something worthwhile?

I recently made a commitment that not only embarrassed me when I found myself unable to fulfill it, but I was further shamed when recognizing the commitment itself had been made in carnal foolishness and presumption. The situation was more than awkward. I felt I was a discredit to the Lord and to the pastoral office I serve in His Name.

I sought God in prayer repentantly. As I did, I felt directed to simply and forthrightly write a letter to all of the parties involved in the situation—and that involved about 500 men!

Without self-defense I acknowledged my misjudgment. I said I couldn't keep my commitment and I asked their forgiveness. But my most challenging assignment was to confess God's showing me how I had acted vainly and stupidly, and I did. I humbly described my unperceived but now recognized pride.

And an amazing thing happened.

Not only did God forgive me, and the men all understand and receive my confession, but a remarkable turnaround in the whole situation occurred. In an occasion that might have been blighted by my failure, God took it and made it into a building block. Before it was over, the triumph that occurred exceeded everyone's brightest expectations.

Only God can do that. Only God can so graciously yet wondrously reverse circumstances caused by our own failures.

And the present ministry of the Holy Spirit is to give rise to your expectation as well, that in spite of whatever has happened to you, He is able to recover, reclaim, restore, renew and rebuild whatever has been broken. He will bring full restoration to your life, your personality, your character, your mind—to whatever part of you has been crushed, bruised, broken, stained, tarnished or ruined.

He can do that and He will. He will do that even when some of the material is the broken pieces of the life you bring Him. So bring your brokenness, no matter what Satan's Sanballatlike suggestions may be. Learn to recognize the Adversary's tactics. He is intent on destroying your confidence that any of these victories can happen. But through the Word, begin to disarm him as you are now aware of his style.

- Whenever he says, "It is never going to get done," don't accept that as a resident thought of your own. It's him—it's the sinister voice of hell.
- When you hear, "It's hopeless; too many things have been broken and burned in the past," define the source at once—it's the devil.
- When you hear *any* kind of innuendo, speak Jesus' words: "Get behind Me, Satan!"[15] Issue your command in the name of Jesus. Then begin to praise and glorify the Lord. He is the One who has sent His Spirit to come to rebuild you—and He's going to do it completely.

Hallelujah! *Hope* is in the breath of the Holy Spirit. *Hope* is yours and mine to keep—and to *know we'll never be embarrassed by God for having hoped in His grace!* (see Romans 5:5)

To cling to hope is to cling to the Lord. Hope is born of the certainty the Holy Spirit wants to instill in us—to *know* God already has the situation in hand. The future is settled in His mind, and...

> *to hope is to embrace the confidence that everything God has promised to be already exists, and all that remains for us to do is to keep walking forward with Him...until we come to the place where each fulfilled promise is already waiting.*

....

Spiritual Workout

1. When you hear of "natural disasters" or other tragedies, do you tend to think first that God or Satan is behind them? What difference does this make?
2. What additional signs of increased evils do you see in our world today?

3. Do you feel you've experienced any of Satan's direct opposition in your own life?
4. Are you aware of any self-defeating "voices" or attitudes that especially arise when you are thinking of launching out on new projects that call for your best?
5. Have you had successes in silencing such voices of doom and gloom that might be an encouragement to share?
6. Are you benefited in any specific ways by regular, faithful worship, or do you often find such services irrelevant to your daily walk?

CHAPTER FIFTEEN

DISCERNING AND DEFEATING THE DEMONIC

The Word:

Nehemiah 4:7,8,11,13,14,16-18,23

Now it happened, when Sanballat, Tobiah, the Arabs, the Ammonites, and the Ashdodites heard that the walls of Jerusalem were being restored and the gaps were beginning to be closed, that they became very angry, and all of them conspired together to come and attack Jerusalem and create confusion.

And our adversaries said, "They will neither know nor see anything, till we come into their midst and kill them and cause the work to cease."

Therefore I positioned men behind the lower parts of the wall, at the openings; and I set the people according to their families, with their swords, their spears, and their bows.

And I looked, and arose and said to the nobles, to the leaders, and to the rest of the people, "Do not be afraid of them. Remember the Lord, great and awesome, and fight for your brethren, your sons, your daughters, your wives, and your houses."

So it was, from that time on, that half of my servants worked at construction, while the other half held the spears, the shields, the bows, and wore armor; and the leaders were behind all the house of Judah. Those who built on the wall, and those who carried burdens, loaded themselves so that with one hand they worked at construction, and with the other held a weapon. Every one of the builders had his sword girded at his side as he built.

So neither I, my brethren, my servants, nor the men of the guard who followed me took off our clothes, except that everyone took them off for washing.

The Target:

- Through seeing Sanballat's marshaling of troops to oppose the rebuilding project, to gain a basic introduction to the nature of Satan's workings through his hosts of demons.
- To recognize this needed understanding for the value of discernment and warfare it is intended to serve, as opposed to curiosity-seeking or mystical pursuits.
- To be apprised of the massively powerful resources we have been given to withstand the Adversary, and to know how to make application of those resources by the power of the Holy Spirit.

DISCERNING AND DEFEATING THE DEMONIC

A discussion about the issues of personal or corporate growth in Christ would not be complete without mention of the demonic realm. The nature and activity of demons really should not be a difficult subject to discuss, because the Bible says so much about it. Jesus was bold and forthright in His dealing with demons, and yet the topic seems to be problematic for some people. Why? There are probably at least three reasons why this is so. As to the subject of demons:

1. It sounds superstitious. In a society that sounds the depths of space with radio-telescopes, explores the solar system with probes and experiments with genetic manipulation in its biology labs, discussing "demons" sounds to some like a retreat to the Dark Ages.

But the truth is that "dark ages" do persist today, not as an era of

DISCERNMENT CAN MAKE THE DIFFERENCE

BETWEEN FIGHTING THE ENEMY

OR CONDEMNING YOURSELF.

unenlightenment, but as one in which the powers of darkness continue their dark workings. Rather than a retreating of works by demons, our age has experienced their renaissance, and there is a growing willingness even on the part of scientists and educators to admit that "something" personal and beyond man is at work around us. A second dimension—an invisible one—is *there*, and evil lurks within that realm.

2. It seems frightening. As with death, disease and war, sensitive people would rather not talk about the subject of demons. Such temerity isn't a matter of adults being "scared," as with a child at a horror movie. It is more like being startled by the realization, upon being awakened at 2:00 A.M., that someone is moving about the house. The presence of a thief is other than "scary," it is terrifying. So is the demonic as frightening, and no better analogy exists, for "the thief" is Jesus' designation for Satan and his ilk, and such similar subjects as mentioned—death, disease and war—are the stock in trade of this evil host. It would be unnatural if the thought of such realities did not increase our adrenaline flow.

3. It becomes exaggerated. It is an unfortunate fact that people make too much or too little of demons. Some mock the notion of their existence; others suspect their presence in a gust of wind or even a sneeze. Some Christians mechanically deny their activities, while others salivate with fanatical excitement at the prospect of conversing about them.

The extremes tend to establish positions, as though Satan himself had spun a centrifuge to force opinion away from the center of mankind's life, leaving demons a wide berth to ply their evil wares with the impunity of an invisible criminal. But in the face of this spread of opinion, our challenge is to face the fact of their presence and activity in the light of God's Word and to deal with them in the power of God's Spirit.

The essential need for recognizing the work of the devil through demonic devices is that the defeat of any adversary must begin by identifying him and discerning his methods of operation. Discernment can make the difference between fighting the Enemy or condemning yourself.

Multiplied hosts of sincere followers of Christ live a lifetime either wrestling with a character deficiency or experiencing recurrent, systematic setbacks after healthy progression. Blaming every failure on themselves, they fail to see the sinister designs of Satan fashioning devices custom-made to obstruct their progress. Sickness, financial reversal, mechanical failure, inner depression, lying suggestions to the mind—are but a few demonic weapons of war.

Of course, not all problems are demonically originated. Some natural explanations are likely in many circumstances. And it is unfortunately also true that much of our opposition often does derive from our flesh, as Walt Kelly said through the lips of his immortal comic character Pogo: "We have met the enemy and he is us!" But there is more to our struggle than "flesh" and "natural circumstance," and that is why understanding and discernment are needed.

A timeless battle is being tirelessly engaged in the invisible realm, and the conflict faced during the quest for Jerusalem's reconstruction in the time of Nehemiah provides significant insight. Here is a clear picture of Satan's patterns of attack with an answering example of principles for our successful resistance.

JUST WHEN THINGS ARE PROGRESSING

Simultaneous with the accomplishment of the walls being rebuilt to half their height, Sanballat and numerous allies are infuriated to the point that they now organize a conspiracy against the builders under Nehemiah's leadership. Their plan is threefold: intimidate, demoralize and defeat. They badger and mock and threaten everything, even death to some and beatings to others, should they attempt to assist the project.

The insidious nature of Satan is present in this pledge to retaliate. There is a complete absence of any justification for Sanballat's hatefulness: only *good* was taking place at Jerusalem; nothing but healthy progress happening among a needy citizenry. But this satanic character cannot tolerate blessing upon people without contesting its continuance:

"We [will] come into their midst and kill them and cause the work to cease."[1]

Nehemiah takes this threat seriously, and the Scriptures record his strategy for defense: (a) he inspires faith, (b) he equips and positions against attack and (c) he presses the work forward.

Again, the narrative's parallel to the practical realities of our personal lives is profoundly impressive. The similarities, both in the dilemmas we face and in the devices the Adversary conjures against us, remind us that others have fought these battles before us. And they have won! We share with those throughout history in an ongoing battle:

> *Therefore we also, since we are surrounded by so great a cloud of witnesses, let us lay aside every weight, and the sin which so easily ensnares us.*[2]

This encouragement springs from a Bible passage recording the names and exploits of others who have fought against evil, progressed against all odds and triumphed by grace through faith. The Word of

---

UNITY NOT ONLY COMFORTS, BUT

ALSO DEFUSES SATANIC PLOTS.

God discloses a dual truth: (a) all these model the faithway of victory; (b) they are witnessing our part in the spiritual struggle and are cheering us on—right now!

We need to do that for each other, too.

You and I need to take notice of Nehemiah's call to the people, "Don't be afraid! Remember the Lord!"[3] Then, he places the people in position "according to their families," a tactic combining sound military strategy with morale-building relationships.

And so with us. The Holy Spirit wants to draw us together and teach us to strengthen each other with mutual encouragement. This unity not only comforts, but also defuses satanic plots "if two...agree" or "where two or three are gathered together"[4] in Jesus' name.

OVERCOMING NOW!

Having been exiled to Patmos as a victim of the spiritual battle, John wrote to the Early Church, "I am your brother and companion in tribulation."[5] It seemed that the powers of the world—both political and spiritual—had neutralized this warrior. But John's awareness of the nature of the conflict makes him a candidate for overcoming and victory. Not only does his writing in the book of Revelation describe the certainty of our ultimate victory over evil, but the existence of the book itself is a study in present triumph.

Apparently confined by an obvious stratagem of hell, John writes about future victory while gaining one at the same time. His example and message reveal that victory is not only a promise of a future conquest, but amid the present struggle victory-unto-victory is also being won right now!

Today's pathway is the same as the one in Revelation. Testifying to Christ's triumph over evil throughout and beyond all history, we are shown the way to overcome evil today—"by the blood of the Lamb and by the word of their testimony."[6]

These weapons—the blood and the Word—are precisely comparable to the armor and the swords Nehemiah provided the builders.

> *So it was, from that time on, that half of my servants worked at construction, while the other half held the spears, the shields, the bows, and wore armor....Every one of the builders had his sword girded at his side as he built.*[7]

Just as Nehemiah did not discount the capacity of Sanballat to succeed in destroying the work and the workers, the New Testament perspective on our Enemy advises serious mindedness: "Be sober, be vigilant; because your adversary the devil walks about like a roaring lion, seeking whom he may devour."[8] There is no reason for us to fear defeat, but neither is there reason for us to doubt there will be battle.

The Bible describes "the armor of God," equipment for spiritual warfare provided by (a) the Cross—"the blood of the Lamb," and applied through (b) the Word of God—"the word of their testimony." Each of these Holy Spirit implements for battle is necessary for both survival and success. The realities of your life and the truth of God's Word recommend complete equipping:

> *Finally, my brethren, be strong in the Lord and in the power of His might. Put on the whole armor of God, that you may be able to stand against the wiles of the devil. For we do not wrestle against flesh and blood, but against principalities, against powers, against the rulers of the darkness of this age, against spiritual hosts of wickedness in the heavenly places.*
>
> *Therefore take up the whole armor of God, that you may be able to withstand in the evil day, and having done all, to stand. Stand therefore, having girded your waist with*

*truth, having put on the breastplate of righteousness, and
having shod your feet with the preparation of the gospel of
peace; above all, taking the shield of faith with which you
will be able to quench all the fiery darts of the wicked one.*

*And take the helmet of salvation, and the sword of the
Spirit, which is the word of God; praying always with all
prayer and supplication in the Spirit, being watchful to
this end with all perseverance and supplication for all the
saints—and for me, that utterance may be given to me,
that I may open my mouth boldly to make known the
mystery of the gospel, for which I am an ambassador in
chains; that in it I may speak boldly, as I ought to speak.*[9]

Stand therefore! The call is clear: *You* put on the armor, and with its
protection—to the use of God's Word as your sword, and the Holy
Spirit's enablement in prayer—you and I *can* defeat demonic assault.

1. Be girded with truth. You cannot battle victoriously if you barter
with the Enemy on his terms. Satan is a liar and the father of *all lying*.
If you become less than truthful, you not only compromise character,
you create problems by allowing the Enemy in your camp. Don't let
him inside the walls! He's a crafty saboteur, ever bent on destruction
even though his deceptive suggestions suggest temporary gain.

How often have you been tempted to use a lie as an assist?

I pastor in a community where a sizable number of people work in
the entertainment industry, where perennial youthfulness often is
proposed as essential to personal acceptance and success. One of my
flock, recently hard put by reason of infrequent work, yielded to the
temptation to lie about age, and even after lying, the actor's agent was
no more successful with casting directors than before.

Time passed. Still no work.

And with passing time, prospects failed until discouragement and
financial distress brought the party to my office. As we talked, I probed
for an answer as to why our earlier prayers had not been answered. It
was in this discussion that the actor confessed to having lied. The force
of Psalm 66:18 came to bear anew as my friend was humbled in repentance. The lie seemed small at first, but "If I regard iniquity in my heart,
the Lord will not hear." We prayed, and this individual made a recom-
mitment to a fresh dependence upon God, without the help of lying.

It's a lesson we must all establish for our walk and our warfare: you can't win against the Liar of liars by lying. Even "white lies" are a lie

YOU CAN'T WIN AGAINST THE
LIAR OF LIARS BY LYING.

by definition. All lying is of the darkness, and we are called to gird against it.

2. Put righteousness on as a breastplate. The ancient warrior wore a heavy breastplate that protected his chest, blunting both sword and spearpoint thrust at him. A similar rain of fire pours forth in the spiritual battle today, seeking to strike through to the heart with volleys of impurity and distraction, enticing us with evil.

These bursts of unrighteousness are not impersonal objects, but are demon attacks—the "fiery darts of the wicked one."[10] Some are diverted by God's intervention, some by the shield of faith, but however quick your footwork, some fiery darts slide by. And it is then that the breastplate of righteousness is put to the test. The question is: What do you do when evil presses against your heart, when every other defense has failed? The breastplate of "right action"—*simply doing right when you know you should*—is crucial to your victory then.

"Keep your heart with all diligence, for out of it spring the issues of life."[11] God not only offers help for overcoming the Enemy, He requires us to join the resistance. He gives the power—you make the choice. So do it. Let right action protect your heart. Stand against wrong when you know you should.

3. Wear the shoes of peace. We have already given considerable study to what our standing is with God through Christ: "We have peace."[12] In Him we have a warrior's stance of surefootedness, steadfastness and unshakable certainty. Our position of "peace with God" is far more than a "feeling," it is a resource for our fighting to keep the peace.

That "footing" is the equipment we are given to advance against and tread down the works of hell. Our position in Christ is not theoretical, it is dynamic. From that stance of confidence we're to move with confidence, move against demonic works and satanic strongholds. Jesus said,

> Behold, I give you the authority to trample on serpents and scorpions, and over all the power of the enemy, and nothing shall by any means hurt you.[13]

The one truly risen and ascended Master in the universe, Jesus the only begotten Son of God, has taken His rightful place, "far above all principality and power and might and dominion, and every name that is named...and He put all things under His feet."[14] Now He directs you and me to wear the shoes gained through His victory. He calls us to march forward without fear.

Walk, don't run. These shoes were made for walkin'...right through the fires of hell's worst attacks.

4. Take the shield of faith and the helmet of salvation. God's promises bring shieldlike faith to repel the Adversary's threats: "Faith comes by hearing, and hearing by the Word of God."[15] That direct statement from Scripture simply condenses to this: If you aren't in the Word, you can't win the war!

Your daily intake of God's Word, allowing the Holy Spirit to arm you through it, is critical to your powers of resistance against the conspiracies of darkness. The shield is as strong in your hand as the Word is in your habit. Take it and faith grows strong—and so do your defenses!

So put on the helmet of salvation.

"We will come in," Sanballat's emissaries threatened.

How like those ancient threats are the demonically inspired thoughts, ideas and mental images that often parade themselves before our minds. Unwelcome, unbidden and sometimes seemingly uncontrolled, they seek to induce the fear, lust, pride and doubt that can lead to despair and defeat. The helmet of salvation is the armor given us against this attack.

HOW DO YOU PUT IT ON?

She stepped into my office, somewhat embarrassed. "Pastor Jack," she asked, "could I talk with you for a minute?"

As she spoke, I was touched by her honesty as she spilled out a sad story of her past life in a perverted lifestyle. Her present frustration was not so much with temptation to return to that life as it was her struggle with a wearying barrage of memories and imaginations from that sorry past.

As we talked, I remembered the Scripture,

> *For the weapons of our warfare are not carnal but mighty in God for pulling down strongholds, casting down arguments and every high thing that exalts itself against the knowledge of God, bringing every thought into captivity to the obedience of Christ.*[16]

I began by explaining that her battle was not against herself. She had felt guilty for even having the thoughts that plagued her, even though she did not welcome them in any way. So from God's Word I taught her, unmasking the real enemy—demons, unclean spirits that were tormenting her mind and lying to her about herself, her past and her present.

Without relating the whole story, when she left my office minutes later she went with a brighter countenance than the distressed, anguished look she wore on arrival. The key turned on her learning how to put on her helmet; learning to take the power of the blood of the Cross that purchased her salvation, and applying its provision to shatter the power of demonic "imaginations" stinging her mind.

Listen! When your mind is bombarded, put your helmet on!

I have encouraged people to literally take their hands while at prayer and put them upon their heads and say: "In the name of Jesus Christ of Nazareth, and by the power of the blood of His cross, I come against every lying, lustful, prideful and hellish spirit. According to God's Word I resist you, and I command you to go. I am a blood-bought child of God! Jesus Christ is my Lord! You are a defeated foe! And I cast down your working now, in Jesus name!"

Don't dabble with the devil. Demand his retreat: "Resist the devil and he will flee from you."[17]

5. Take the sword of the Spirit...with all prayer. God's Word is not only a resource for faith that defends against the devil, it is a weapon for attack—and *prayer is the means by which this sword is wielded.* Ephesians 6:17,18 says:

> *And take...the sword of the Spirit, which is the word of God; praying always with all prayer and supplication in the Spirit.*

Two things will help you if you will take the sword of the Spirit and retaliate, determined that it is not enough just to stand firm in defense, but ready to launch an offensive!

First, your prayer does not have to be lengthy. This is no argument against extended devotional or intercessory prayer. But in the midst of the spiritual struggle, the Holy Spirit will at times give clear insights for prayer. When He does, stop there—and use it. Go to prayer at once as a commanding officer firing a retaliatory ballistic missile against an encroaching adversary. Thrust into Satan's domain with the Spirit's sword.

Second, understand how that sword is applied to prayer. Thrusts with the sword of God's Word are accomplished as the Holy Spirit brings promises or principles from the Word to mind; ones which apply to your present struggle. "Praying in the Spirit" involves several modes of expression, but primary among them is the declaration of God's eternal Word against the devil. Jesus retaliated against Satan time and again, saying, "It is written...it is written," and the same method forces the retreat of hell's powers today.

The combination of God's promises joined to Holy Spirit-prompted prayer is an invincible resource. The spiritual struggle is real; demons are not imaginary. Satan is at work, but that is not the whole story. The final truth is this: You can stand! You can win! And you can launch a triumphant counterattack!

Prayer is the means by which we invade territory held by the Adversary and wrench from him the souls, the possessions, the fields of activity and the tools of destruction he presently dominates and utilizes. Holy Spirit-inspired and-enabled prayer is the potential of every Spirit-filled believer, but you cannot attack unless you pray.

A CONCLUDING WORD

Nehemiah's direction and equipping of the Jerusalemites for resistance and victory displays timeless principles:

- The Enemy is real, not imaginary.

- The battle is crucial; defeat or victory is at stake.
- Victory is certain when God's people draw on His resources.

The Holy Spirit is your ever-present Comforter; with you today to show the way to secure the "city" of your own soul and personal circumstances and bring victory against every satanic onslaught.

Spiritual warfare is no game, but neither is it a realm to fear or attempt to avoid. There is no escaping its reality and no running from its implications. People who deny it or philosophize about it are already victims of the battle: They have been taken captive by the deluding spirit of the world.

Paul spoke of the Adversary's tactics saying, "We are not ignorant of his devices," noting that where such ignorance prevails Satan gains a distinct advantage.[18]

One final note before leaving this passage: An almost casual mention is made of the fact that the vigilance of the people was so constant that no one took off their clothes "except...for washing."[19] What might pass as a matter of insignificant reference contains an important point of counsel for us all:

Never become so consumed with the struggle that you neglect attention to your daily, personal cleansing before the Lord.

Preoccupation with warfare to the neglect of fellowship and devotion with Christ can breed an insensitive, forgetful builder. And that creates another kind of problem—one which happened with the people Nehemiah was assisting.

SPIRITUAL WORKOUT

1. Do you tend to credit Satan with the power to personally attack believers, or do you think of his influence as more abstract and general? Are there reasons for this besides those suggested in this chapter?
2. Share with the group any experiences in your own life that indicate direct demonic attack.
3. Read Revelation 12:9-12. What target did Satan single out

here? Do you see any evidence of this in our nation today?

4. Of the five pieces of the armor of God—truth, righteous-ness, peace, faith and prayer—which do you sense you need to give more attention to "putting on"?

5. Do you have a daily private time with God through prayer and the Word? If not, what would it take for you to adopt this discipline?

6. Do you think men, or "the men's movement," are vulnera-ble to any specific attacks from Satan and his forces?

CHAPTER SIXTEEN

Built Up to Grow Up

The Word:

Nehemiah 5:1-6

And there was a great outcry of the people and their wives against their Jewish brethren.

For there were those who said, "We, our sons, and our daughters are many; therefore let us get grain, that we may eat and live."

There were also some who said, "We have mortgaged our lands and vineyards and houses, that we might buy grain because of the famine."

There were also those who said, "We have borrowed money for the king's tax on our lands and vineyards. Yet now our flesh is as the flesh of our brethren, our children as their children; and indeed we are forcing our sons and our daughters to be slaves, and some of our daughters have been brought into slavery already. It is not in our power to redeem them, for other men have our lands and vineyards."

And I became very angry when I heard their outcry and these words.

The Target:

- To see how Nehemiah's return visit, following an extensive visit away from Jerusalem, illustrates the Holy Spirit's insistence that we learn to live in an accountable responsiveness and responsibility to what He builds or rebuilds in us.
- To examine specific categories of responsibility; not as a composition of legalistic lists, but as a means of recognizing significant issues that are commonly neglected.
- To confront the possibility of our flesh to submit to satanic ploys, in the same way the people of Jerusalem gave "space" to Tobiah. Addressing that issue through refusing to "give place to the devil" (Eph. 4:27).

Built Up to Grow Up

One grand feature of God's economy that is much more difficult to receive than redemptive restoration is the acceptance of our own responsibility. It's always nicer to hear about God's grace than about our duty.

Our progress in restoration is measured more and more by our capacity to accept responsibility, because as precious as God's patience and loving-kindness is, He is also set on growing us up. This means we must come to terms with areas of our own failure, where duty and discipline on our part are required. We're not dealing with reconstruction now; we're dealing with life in the rebuilt city.

One of the great ways God is moving among men today is in securing patterns of accepted responsibility. Nothing is more thrilling than to stand shoulder to shoulder with men who have made up their minds to do their personal part in stemming the tide of irresponsible behavior that has flooded this country for a full generation.

Can we face up to the sad indictments? Males in general must confront the fact that they have sown their procreative seeds willy-nilly, producing children without the advantage of fathers; been unfaithful to their spouses to a degree that is disproportionate to the number of unfaithful wives; and created an infamous national crime statistic in the area of defaulting in child support. Yet the Christian men's movement has risen like a beacon in a gale against this tide of irresponsibility, calling men to shoulder courageously the responsibility of love and faithfulness and duty.

Have you committed your own wholehearted support of this modern revolution in gallantry?

Any sensitive teacher hesitates pressing the point of requirements, not only because he prefers not sounding legalistic, but also because the human psyche is so guilt-prone anyway. For my part, I want to teach responsibility, but I want to motivate by love rather than by guilt. Guilt.

That old saw, "You are your own worst enemy," rips into all our consciences with such frequent justice that it's small wonder we sometimes feel the need to apologize to God for getting up in the morning. How often my own dullness and disobedience have prompted my quoting Dizzy Dean's famous lament, "I shoulda stood in bed!"

DEPENDENT RESPONSIBILITY

God's call to responsibility is a challenging matter for us to address, because in growing to understand it we must walk a line of delicate balance. On the one hand, God's insistence on our accepting our own responsibility is not a resignation on His part from His will to love, provide, sustain and empower. On the other hand, our acceptance of fuller assignments and duty as we are renewed and are growing in Christ is not a presumption that we have outgrown our place of dependence upon Him.

The story in Jerusalem presents a practical case of this balance between dependence and responsibility. The rebuilding program was moving toward completion. Things were looking great! Huge segments of the wall now stood silhouetted against the sky as testimonies to God's faithfulness, Nehemiah's leadership and the people's responsible participation. Apparently all that remained to be done was to finish some stonework on the walls, to be followed shortly by the building and hanging of the great gates.

Sanballat and Tobiah were not yet silenced, but they were rendered ineffective; their threats, mockings and conspiratorial designs had all been resisted and overthrown.

But suddenly, an outcry rises. "And there was a great outcry of the people and their wives against their...brethren."[1] The ensuing analysis of their complaint discloses one selfish, stupid action after another on the part of the people themselves, revealing behavior that was on the verge of defeating the project from within, after outside enemies had been so successfully resisted.

At the risk of sounding insensitive, impatient and even unloving, let me take two chapters and bluntly confront you with them. In communicating the good news of God's almighty grace and kindness, we are unfaithful to the truth if we fail to acknowledge the point of the gospel. God's desire is to make all of us whole to the point that we are *able* to function in the independence wholeness allows, as people who choose to walk in the childlikeness that humility requires. This state means being able to get along alone while remaining wise enough to know we need Him—and one another.

Of course such "independence" and "getting along alone" are only relative, because no created being is ever completely self-sufficient. God is our source of breath, of life, of provision, of grace and of all that enables the accomplishing of His highest will. But there is a sweeping difference between our dependency upon Him during the winter of our desperation and recovery from our destructions, and during the summer of our growth into fruitfulness in the sunshine of His life and power. As we come to that season, He will require more of us than before, not because we are independently capable, but because He, our Creator, has now restored us to the capacity for responsible self-rule under His overarching government in our souls.

DISCIPLINED ACCOUNTABILITY

Jerusalem was in disarray.

Chapter 5 shows the people in debt, being eaten up by taxes, their children being put into slavery to pay debts, families at one another's throats—and Nehemiah is mad!

I love Nehemiah's capacity for anger. Because he prefigures the Holy Spirit, some would conceivably suppose the prophet to be incapable of plain, assertive, forthright indignation. But this capacity is not inconsistent with the Holy Spirit Himself, for He is not only characterized by the gentleness of a dove, but also as the Spirit of judgment and burning: "For our God is a consuming fire."[2] The Holy Spirit not only can be resisted, grieved and sinned against; He is also quite able to respond: "But they rebelled and grieved His Holy Spirit; so He turned Himself against them as an enemy, and He fought against them."[3]

When I say, "I love Nehemiah's capacity for anger," and note how the Word of God reveals the same trait in the Holy Spirit's dealings, it is important to understand the context prompting that remark. To study the previously cited passages that show the Holy Spirit rising in indignation, we find even then that His anger and action seek the ultimate good of the people involved. His assertive vengeance is never vindictive, but confrontational and bold to judge against evil. He won't stand for it, nor will He allow us to willfully, ignorantly push forward unto our own confusion or failure. Because He cares enough to restore us, He cares enough to confront us. His loving tenderness does not preempt a potent readiness to discipline.

A MAN'S MAN CAN BE AGGRESSIVE AND BOLD AND FORTHRIGHT; AND AT ONCE TENDER AND LOVING.

(Incidentally, Nehemiah, as a picture of the Holy Spirit at work in building us as men, reveals something of what a man's man might look like, living out God's vision for men. He can be aggressive and bold and forthright; and at once tender and loving. It's a combination that often reminds me of an ad campaign Kleenex conducted, featuring the cartoon figure of a jut-jawed, brawny guy on the box, with the caption, "Tough, but oh so gentle.")

In chapter 13 is a second case of Nehemiah's same aggressive manner as he deals with irresponsibility and disobedience among the people. The first case was just before the gates are hung and the wall dedicated. The second is sometime after Nehemiah had completed the project, resumed his post in Persia and had returned for a brief visit to Jerusalem. On both occasions the failures distill to two categories: (a) mismanagement of finances and (b) insensitivity in relationships, both resulting from general disobedience to explicit practical laws of God.

Nehemiah's visit is shocking to the point of being humorous—that is, as long as you weren't the recipient of his correction! Nehemiah describes that upon return he discovers that refuge has been given to the evil Tobiah—and in the Temple itself of all places! Other compromises had been made in his absence, and he moves with bold and deliberate dispatch.

> Eliashib the priest, who had been appointed as custodian
> of the Temple storerooms and who was also a good friend
> of Tobiah, had converted a storage room into a beautiful

guest room for Tobiah. The room had previously been used for storing the grain offerings, frankincense, bowls, and tithes of grain, new wine, and olive oil....

I was not in Jerusalem at the time, for I had returned to Babylon in the thirty-second year of the reign of King Artaxerxes (though I later received his permission to go back again to Jerusalem). When I arrived back in Jerusalem and learned of this evil deed of Eliashib—that he had prepared a guest room in the Temple for Tobiah—I was very upset and threw out all of his belongings from the room. Then I demanded that the room be thoroughly cleaned, and I brought back the Temple bowls, the grain offerings, and frankincense.

I also learned that the Levites had not been given what was due them, so they and the choir singers who were supposed to conduct the worship services had returned to their farms. I immediately confronted the leaders and demanded, "Why has the Temple been forsaken?" Then I called all the Levites back again and restored them to their proper duties. And once more all the people of Judah began bringing their tithes of grain, new wine, and olive oil to the Temple treasury....

One day I was on a farm and saw some men treading winepresses on the Sabbath, hauling in sheaves, and loading their donkeys with wine, grapes, figs, and all sorts of produce which they took that day into Jerusalem. So I opposed them publicly. There were also some men from Tyre bringing fish and all sorts of wares and selling them on the Sabbath to the people of Jerusalem.

Then I asked the leaders of Judah, "Why are you profaning the Sabbath? Wasn't it enough that your fathers did this sort of thing and brought the present evil days upon us and upon our city? And now you are bringing more wrath upon the people of Israel by permitting the Sabbath to be desecrated in this way."

So from then on I commanded that the gates of the city be shut as darkness fell on Friday evenings and not be opened until the Sabbath had ended; and I sent some of my servants to guard the gates so that no merchandise could be brought in on the Sabbath day. The merchants and trades- men camped outside Jerusalem once or twice, but I spoke sharply to them and said, "What are you doing out here, camping around the wall? If you do this again, I will arrest you." And that was the last time they came on the Sabbath....

About the same time I realized that some of the Jews had married women from Ashdod, Ammon, and Moab, and that many of their children spoke in the language of Ashdod and couldn't speak the language of Judah at all. So I argued with these parents and cursed them and punched a few of them and knocked them around and pulled out their hair; and they vowed before God that they would not let their children intermarry with non-Jews.

"Wasn't this exactly King Solomon's problem?" I demanded. "There was no king who could compare with him, and God loved him and made him the king over all Israel; but even so he was led into idolatry by foreign women. Do you think that we will let you get away with this sinful deed?"

One of the sons of Jehoiada (the son of Eliashib the High Priest) was a son-in-law of Sanballat the Horonite, so I chased him out of the Temple. Remember them, O my God, for they have defiled the priesthood and the promis- es and vows of the priests and Levites. So I purged out the foreigners, and assigned tasks to the priests and Levites, making certain that each knew his work.[4]

Wow! What more can you say?

Nehemiah was *serious* about the subject of responsibility. He required the people to maintain their lives and their city under divine govern- ment. This text clearly teaches how the goal of any restoration program God has is to beget responsible self-government instead of slothful self- indulgence. The Holy Spirit wants the Jerusalem of your life to be a city of the great King—one where His Kingdom life is lived and served.

Numerous details might be analyzed within each of these two chap- ters, each relating to factors so frequently hindering the growth of sin- cere believers today:

1. They were financially overextended and victims of economic frustration. Their concern for their children's being fed is commendable, but it was manifesting in strife, discord and interpersonal conflict.[5]
2. This occasioned financial decisions that seemed necessary but that were only creating deeper problems. Mortgaging property or deferring of tax payments to ease financial pressure was only a stopgap solution that was now coming back to haunt them.[6]
3. Amid the pressures of life, children who were earlier the source of concern now become the objects of slavery, merchandised under pressure in order to meet their debtors' demands.[7]
4. Contrary to the Levitical law, they were demanding exorbitant interest of one another (usury). Their relationships to one another were thereby devalued, and the result was strain among brethren and deepening of debt.
5. Mixed marriages reflected something other than social openness; they showed an indifference to God's order that His people be separate from the world.[8]
6. Entertaining Tobiah was far different than a social courtesy; it involved an absence of discernment concerning the nature of evil and it issued a welcome to the abiding presence of a decadent influence at the heart of their spiritual experience.[9]
7. Spiritual leadership was uncared for by the people and thereby their effectiveness reduced; a problem that indicated more than insensitive neglect, but was due to disobedience in their financial program of giving.[10]
8. Sabbath violation was rampant, practice that not only disobeyed the law of God, as violation of needed rest always does; life becomes counterproductive, and material interests prevail over spiritual ones.[11]

DETERMINED INFIDELITY

It is of supreme importance that we understand that Nehemiah's anger was not merely over the acts of disobedience and foolishness. It was primarily over the fact that these same people had made specific commitments not to do the things they were now doing.

These were not acts of ignorance. They knew better. Moreover, they had confessed with repentance and regret, having walked in such past disobedience. Chapter 9 elaborates their repentance in the light of God's great mercy and grace, and chapter 10 lists the names of those who led in sealing a covenant of obedience to walk according to God's law.

But now Nehemiah discovers their retreat from that covenant, and he refuses to allow them to violate their commitment to God. His anger is not against them, but is to shock and shake them back to that place where their best interests will be served through fidelity toward the Lord.

Years of pastoring have taught me that the healing and deliverance of human souls is only preservable where responsible obedience is manifest by those receiving the Holy Spirit's rebuilding within them. Nehemiah's anger and action are fully appropriate, and should be taken to reveal God's heart concerning known violation of foundational principles taught in His Word.

Jesus' words to the restored so often include the requirement for responsible follow-through that we are wise to hear His voice.

- Behold, you are made whole: sin no more lest a worse thing come upon you.[12]
- When an unclean spirit goes out of a man, he goes through dry places, seeking rest; and finding none, he says, "I will return to my house from which I came." And when he comes, he finds it swept and put in order. Then he goes and takes with him seven other spirits more wicked than himself, and they enter and dwell there; and the last state of that man is worse than the first.[13]
- Neither do I condemn you; go and sin no more.[14]

These are hard words.

DEDICATED SENSITIVITY

Nothing is so pointed as the issues of discipleship once a person has been reborn by God's grace, recovered by His merciful Spirit and equipped by the resources of His Word. Now we are nearing the conclusion of this study on the tender mercies of God's Spirit, meeting us in our brokenness and bringing us to wholeness.

And I am concerned.

I don't want to conclude in a manner that stultifies an earnest soul with a condemning fear, just as you are beginning to regain confidence and hope. Don't let these words about duty and discipline work against your faith in God's high purpose for your life. Perfection isn't a demand, but it is a goal—and the essence of walking the pathway toward that objective is in keeping a heart open to the Holy Spirit. He will only require obedience of you at those points He has already taught you. But you must keep sensitive to His voice, just as surely as you must walk obediently to His counsel.

Responsibility means "your ability to respond," and where your understanding has been enlightened, your bondage to the past broken and your commitment fully declared, He will expect you to walk as a child of the light.

The way to do so is to know the heart of God through His Word. That Word not only commands obedience, but the heart of that Word invites you to a pathway of joy and fulfillment that will make obedience both livable and enjoyable.

The key to living the life the Comforter wants us to live is in learning to receive the Word of God with understanding, peace and joy.

Let's see how that can be done—constantly, joyously.

SPIRITUAL WORKOUT

1. As you have studied this chapter, what issue neglected by the Jerusalemites most troubles you about them? What of their reversion to irresponsible maintenance of what God had given them seems to most address something in your own life?

2. Can you recall the first time in your life when you experienced the necessity of being more responsible, or to take on more duty, than is expected of a child? What memories, associations, or feelings are connected in your mind with the word "duty"? What special responsibilities does God ask you as a spouse or a parent to take on?

3. What special responsibilities do you find as a Christian man in the world of work? What special resources do Christians have to meet these demands?
4. Does Nehemiah's model of the Holy Spirit's passion—even jealous anger over us—surprise you?
5. Are you aware of any circumstances where you need to stand more boldly against falsehood or ungodly practices?

CHAPTER SEVENTEEN

Facing Tomorrow with Joy

The Word:

Nehemiah 8:1-10

Now all the people gathered together as one man in the open square that was in front of the Water Gate; and they told Ezra the scribe to bring the Book of the Law of Moses, which the Lord had commanded Israel. So Ezra the priest brought the Law before the assembly of men and women and all who could hear with understanding on the first day of the seventh month. Then he read from it in the open square that was in front of the Water Gate from morning until midday, before the men and women and those who could understand; and the ears of all the people were attentive to the Book of the Law.

So Ezra the scribe stood on a platform of wood which they had made for the purpose....And Ezra opened the book in the sight of all the people, for he was standing above all the people; and when he opened it, all the people stood up. And Ezra blessed the Lord, the great God. Then all the people answered, "Amen, Amen!" while lifting up their hands. And they bowed their heads and worshiped the Lord with their faces to the ground....And the Levites, helped the people to understand the Law; and the people stood in their place. So they read distinctly from the book, in the Law of God; and they gave the sense, and helped them to understand the reading.

And Nehemiah, who was the governor, Ezra the priest and scribe, and the Levites who taught the people said to all the people, "This day is holy to the Lord your God; do not mourn nor weep." For all the people wept, when they heard the words of the Law.

Then he said to them, "Go your way, eat the fat, drink the sweet, and send portions to those for whom nothing is prepared; for this day is holy to our Lord. Do not sorrow, for the joy of the Lord is your strength."

The Target:

- To point to the pathway of joy as a means of abiding in the strength of the Lord.
- To show how living a life of humility, availability to correction, and an ongoingly repentant spirit is not to yield to a life of guilt, discouragement or condemnation—rather, to continued, joyous growth.
- To secure in our minds the confidence of God's continued pleasure with us as His redeemed, and His promised commitment to continual development—Being *built* by the Spirit is to set the pathway for timeless *growth* in His way, by His power.

Facing Tomorrow with Joy

———❧———

Breathe deeply. Do it again, please.

Now, touch the most solid object near you, and answer this question: Which is the most substantial and significant—the breath of life or the things around us?

Simple to answer, isn't it? Life is.

Next question: In the biological realm, where does the breath of life draw its power to sustain?

Answer: From the elements that constitute our atmosphere, as they interact with the breathing organism.

Last question: In the ultimate analysis, where does all life find its source and sustaining power?

Answer: From the breath of God that is infused with His Word, which He speaks to create and support, to redeem and sustain.

This quiz is more than academic.

I'm trying to find a way to help deepen sensitivity to the truth that God's voice—*His Word breathed to you*—is the quintessence of your being and your becoming. I'm seeking some means to describe God's Word as *life*, rather than its seeming to be only a book—however wonderful and grand.

To Touch Eternity Today

Please think with me further.

Consider the one thing in this world that you and I can touch that has "eternity" written into its fabric. It's the Word of God. Now, think on this: Every time I take a Bible in hand, I hold eternity, because the life-force inherent in that Word exceeds all time and space: *"Heaven and earth will pass away, but My Word shall not pass away."*[1]

Pause to slowly speak those words above. Pensively allow them to engrave themselves on your soul, for they hold the seeds of the deepest, grandest point of understanding any human being can ever gain.

Your life becomes durable, fulfilling and successful in direct proportion to the degree the Word of God becomes alive to your being, life, breath as healing and creative power.

I'm concerned now with the substantial. I'm concerned with the stuff of life. And the Word of God is *that*: the source of all substance, the source of all life. *"In the beginning God created"*[2]—He did that with His Word. "In the beginning was the Word"[3]—Christ was there at creation. These two facts weld into one, helping us understand the eternal truth:

> *All that is and shall be flows to man by Jesus Christ*
> *through the Word of God!*

That's why my consuming concern has prompted my reserving Nehemiah 8 for our final point of study. It is the record of a people *rediscovering* the Word of God, *misunderstanding* it, *responding* exactly backwards and then *being helped* by Nehemiah to a God-intended response to His Law.

I want to do my utmost to ensure that you know how to keep on receiving the Word of God. I don't mean how to read it, how to memorize it or how to study it, though all of those practices are very important. My primary concern is that in your use of the Word, its *life*, breath and intent—the very *spirit* of the Word—will fill and fulfill your soul continually. It's the only way to keep the "rebuilt you" built up and expanding.

The Word of God is not simply words, information, facts and black-print-on-white pages. It is eternal, durable, life-giving, healing, protecting and dynamically invincible. It will last.

And that's why I want to press the point of your knowing how to let it work in you, for "Here, in His Word, God has given such great and priceless promises...and if their real meaning is at work in you, there is no way you'll ever be less than filled with life and fruitful living."[4]

THE PROBLEM WITH "RECEIVING"

Preliminary to the dedication of the completed walls, Nehemiah enlisted the help of Ezra the priest to present the Word of God to all the people. A two-day event was scheduled and logistical arrangements made, including preparation of a high platform from which the readers and teachers could more easily be seen by everyone.

Because we're so accustomed to it, we can hardly appreciate our privilege in each having our own Bibles. The people of Nehemiah's day did, of course, live so long before the advent of the printing press. Scrolls of the Law were rare, and something of the preciousness of the Word to those ancient people is evident in their praiseful response to Ezra's rising to open the Book.

They worship and give thanks, lifting up their hands in praise, and then they remain standing together for several hours, just to hear God's Word. Whether bowing or lifting hands, whether standing respectfully or listening attentively, the whole scene is one of gratitude and reverence for the Word of God. It was a thrilling day, and adding to it all was the careful explanation given by those who "gave the sense" of what had been clearly read from the Law, helping the people understand the meaning.

Brothers, there is a point of admonition to you and me. *We men need to respond with forthrightness and openness to the Holy Spirit, in worship and praise, with both understanding and emotional sensitivity.* Let's none of us allow ourselves to be fooled at this point by all the talk about "male-female" differences. All the talk about "right brain/left brain"—about "women are from Venus and men from Mars"—may hold an insight or two. But the ultimate issue for you and me is to allow the Holy Spirit to restore, to build and to move upon us as *whole* men.

In the text, the people are both emotionally moved and rationally instructed; they both worship and learn as Nehemiah and Ezra present the precious Word of God. We are wise to learn to show the same availability, as the Holy Spirit moves upon us—through the Word and by His presence.

A SUDDEN TURN

Then a sudden turn occurs. What began so joyously suddenly reverses. People began to weep mournfully. Apparently, as they heard the words of the Law of God, they were overwhelmed, both men and women, by feelings of their own violations of the Word and their inadequacy to fulfill it. The situation was one most church leaders would revel in—a repentant, sensitive response to the awareness that God's commands had been neglected. Here was obvious fruit of awakened understanding of passionate concern.

Or was it?

The absolutely amazing thing about this whole incident is that both Nehemiah and Ezra *stop* this demonstration. They speak correctively

---

THE PROCESS OF UNFOLDING THE SCRIPTURES

IS INTENDED TO ISSUE IN OUR JOY.

---

to the people, insisting that because "this is a holy day," mourning and weeping are inappropriate.

It is mind-boggling! Here is a total reversal of expected religious tradition. And then, as though stopping tears of repentance isn't enough, the two leaders begin to stir the people toward celebration: "Go your way, eat the fat, drink the sweet, and send portions to those for whom nothing is prepared; for this day is holy to our Lord."[5]

Incredible! It's like a party in the name of God; one that started that very day and then progressed to a full scale, week-long observance of the ancient Feast of Tabernacles!

This narrative contains a staggering revelation! Leaping from this episode is a mighty statement about God's heart toward the way we receive His Word. The message is implicit. The process of unfolding the Scriptures is intended to issue in our joy.

What should we think of this?

We must not overlook the fact that even though a feast of rejoicing was urged by Ezra and Nehemiah, the following chapter, Nehemiah 9, is dedicated entirely to the record of the people's confession of sin, with fasting and manifest repentance. This fact makes clear there was nothing shallow in Nehemiah's summons to celebrate, as though he were promoting a glib response to God's Law.

Yet perhaps there is something of equal clarity we are to see. Could it be that his action, set forth so dramatically, is intended to help us understand something about how God would *prefer* our response to His revelation to be? Is this story a lesson in which God is saying, "I want your *first* response to my Word to be one of joyous hope"? I think so. Here again, we men must confront the question of whether our nature or our conditioning in the often unfeeling world of business and manual labor inhibits our capacity to be demonstrative and to express sheer joy and delight, as the people here are urged to do.

It appears that in Nehemiah's counsel to this throng, so beset with shame over their awareness of the contradiction between their practice and God's commands, that God would have us learn to rejoice in hope as well as to repent in contrition. Such a proposition makes spiritual sense for at least two reasons:

1. It emphasizes the element of promise inherent in the corrective Word of Truth. In other words, if I recognize my life doesn't measure up to God's Word, and if I choose to obey His will, I can begin by rejoicing. Knowing the "promise power" in the commandments, I can rejoice that the same Word that rebukes me will also release me! The Law that guides me will also fuel my soul with a dynamic for living! Several texts support this truth:

> "Faithful is He who calls you, who also will do it"[6]; a promise that when God gives an assignment to us, His words include enablement.

> "For no word of God is without power."[7] This verse, translated elsewhere "For with God nothing will be impossible," is a mighty affirmation that contained in every word God speaks is the power needed to actuate it; the very Word directing behavior develops it.

> This is why Paul assures the Philippians, "It is God who works in you both to will and to do for His good pleasure."[8]

2. It builds repentance upon the foundation of faith and decisive commitment, rather than upon guilt and emotionalism. This value is revealed in the way the Corinthians were commended for genuine repentance based on more than humanistic remorse:

> *For godly sorrow produces repentance leading to salvation,
> not to be regretted; but the sorrow of the world produces
> death. For observe this very thing, that you sorrowed in a
> godly manner: What diligence it produced in you, what
> clearing of yourselves, what indignation, what fear, what
> vehement desire, what zeal, what vindication! In all things
> you proved yourselves to be clear in this matter.*[9]

The godly repentance shown in Nehemiah 9, following the feasting and rejoicing counseled by their leaders, verifies that a joyous response to God's Word is not adverse to a repentant spirit, but complementary to it.

In His parable of the sower,[10] Jesus spoke of people receiving the Word with gladness. The fact that His story describes these as cases where shallowness of soul brought no abiding fruit doesn't imply the "gladness" was at fault, but their "having no depth" was. In other words, depth and joyousness can go together.

Philip's preaching in Samaria resulted in the entire city's being filled with great joy.[11] And this is not surprising. The gospel is good news, and there is only one logical response to such tidings!

THE COMFORT OF THE COMFORTER

Several years ago, a new understanding began to dawn on my soul. I was seeking the Lord for guidance concerning my own pastoral teaching ministry, and inquiring of Him specifically concerning the mood and manner of our congregation's worship services.

For much of my life, reverence at worship was basically defined as "silence," and the expected sign of God's presence with power was "uncomfortable sinners"—people squirming under conviction.

Of course, I had seen times when His awesome presence inspired me to "Be still, and know that [He is] God,"[12] and I had also seen sinners cringe as the sword of the Spirit pierced their souls. The general opinion seemed to be that God intended these manifestations to be normative.

Although silence usually prevailed, worship also was usually perfunctory. And though souls were born again, few were saved by reason of having been gripped in a vise of inner conviction. The irregularity of what took place challenged my notion of its being normal worship.

I began to ask, "Just what, Lord, *should* be the atmosphere among a people who worship You and where Your Word is faithfully preached?"

While at prayer about this matter, I sensed God answering me from His own Word: "Comfort, yes, comfort My people!...Speak comfort to Jerusalem, and cry out to her, that her warfare is ended."[13]

The more I thought about this and studied the context of Isaiah's prophecy, I began to see the sunlight of a truth I had never quite perceived before: *God wants people to be happy in His presence!* The continued call throughout the Psalms is to praise and rejoice before the Lord: "In Your presence is fullness of joy; at Your right hand are pleasures forevermore."[14] In the same spirit, Paul insists of the Philippians: "Rejoice in the Lord always: and again I say, Rejoice."[15]

The result of my quest was a slow but definite transformation in my approach to leading our services. It wasn't as though I had been negative or dismal, but I invited and modeled a new brightness. It was not a superficial promotionalism, but an atmosphere birthed by the confidence that when we are happy in His presence, it makes Him happy too!

I soon found people responded with greater faith and commitment, and they steadily moved forward in more definitive growth and service. Not only were our services healthy times of celebration in worship and the Word, but hearts and homes began to flourish in the sunlight of God's love and joy. Somehow, without our realizing it at the time, Ezra and Nehemiah's instruction was being lived out among a people—men and women alike—who were beginning to learn the wisdom of receiving the Word of God with joy.

Today, when repentance is needed (and so often it is) we repent; when a new call to holiness is issued, we obey; when the depths of our hearts are plumbed, sensitive response is shown. But the predominant atmosphere is one of sound-minded, balanced joyfulness, and the biblical fruit of that joy is seen everywhere: "For the joy of the Lord is your strength!"[16]

REJOICE IN HIS WORD

Joy is the pulse beat to the heart of the message that has resounded since the birth of Christ: "Behold, I bring you good tidings of great joy that shall be unto all people, for unto you this day is born a Savior, which is Christ the Lord."[17]

The news is good:	"I bring you *good tidings*
The joy is great:	of *great joy* to all people
The focus is you:	for unto *you*
The time is now:	*this day* is born a Savior
And God is here:	which is *Christ the Lord*!"

Dear friend, I want to send you into all your tomorrows with the Word of God in your hand and the joy of the Lord in your heart. *Yes,* His Word is absolute authority and, yes, He absolutely calls us to obedience in following Jesus Christ. Nothing is silly here. But joy is appropriate when that same Word is received and that joy becomes strength to your soul. When you have said, "Yes, Lord" to His Word, there is

—◆—

THE WORD THAT CREATED ALL WORLDS IS THE WORD THAT IS COMPLETING YOU. SO REST IN THAT ASSURANCE AND REJOICE IN HIS WORD....

—◆—

every reason to begin rejoicing at once. We need not wait until perfection is secured, for His welcomed Word will work progressively and mightily in you to accomplish the Father's pleasure. And you can rejoice *now* over that!

Your growth and furtherance in every part of life is dependent upon, extended and sustained by God's Spirit working the sheer power and freeing truth of His Word in you. The Word that created all worlds is the Word that is completing you. So rest in that assurance and rejoice in His Word as He teaches, shapes and corrects. It's His true intent for your response to His Word.

Centuries ago, a band of battered people stood facing the embarrassing evidence of their inability to recover the ruins of their past.

Then a man came.

With marvelous tenderness, abundant supply and patient persistence, He taught them to pray, to resist adversity and attacks from their enemies. And he brought them to the completion of their goal.

Then one day he led them in the searching out of the full counsel of God's Word. And as they discovered their deficiencies they mourned, until this man rose to declare: "This is a day of God's holy delight: Stop mourning. Rejoice! For the joy of the Lord shall be your strength."

Don't miss seeing Him. He's there in that story, and He's here today. He's the Holy Spirit.

He's here as you read these words; here to take you from this moment onward unto the fulfillment of all of the Father's high destiny for you.

Rebirth, redemption, restoration and recovery are only a part of His mission. He wants to bring you to full *realization* as well; the realization of God's purposes, patterns and promises for your life.

You'll find them all in His Word.

And if you'll allow the Holy Spirit to teach you that Word, He'll help you to continually receive God's precious Word with faith, hope, obedience—and with joy. He will enable you not only to experience joy personally, down deep in your soul, but your interaction with other men and women in God's family will take on a new texture of gladness.

You can walk into tomorrow rejoicing in the warm delight that God's commitment to His purpose in you is absolutely complete. And you can live every day with confidence, assured of the inevitability of His Word triumphing in you.

··

SPIRITUAL WORKOUT

1. Take time to summarize the basic features of your study through Nehemiah.
2. Review the "pictorial characters": Nehemiah is like? Sanballat is like? The Temple, walls, city, region are like?
3. What features of this final chapter most capture your heart and bring joyous expectancy?
4. What steps do you want to take, with others' involvement, to maintain an accountable application of what you have gained through this study?

APPENDICES

WHERE IS NEHEMIAH IN HISTORY?

One probable reason the book of Nehemiah is generally bypassed in study is that the average Bible reader has difficulty envisioning its historic placement. Beside the fact it contains several censuses (7:4-73; 11:1-36; 12:1-26), genealogies (12:1-26), uninviting passages with difficult names listed (3:1-32; 12:32-47) or the apparent redundant recitation of history recorded elsewhere (9:5-38), most readers do not know where it fits in history. The following time line and brief remarks are intended to help orientate you to the place of Nehemiah in Bible history.

Historical Notes	Historical Time Line	

1. Babylon held world dominance for a very short time (c. 605-539 B.C.), but Nebuchadnezzar, the king who gained that dominance, was the instrument God used to judge Judah (Southern Kingdom) and bring about the destruction of Jerusalem. The fall of Babylon took place under Nebuchadnezzar's grandson, Belshazzar, by an overthrow—an engineering/military tactic of phenomenal proportion—executed in one night according to Daniel's prophecy (see Dan. 5). The overthrow was accomplished by Cyrus the Medo-Persian leader.

Abraham	c. 2000
Isaac	c. 1950
Jacob (to Egypt)	c. 1830
Moses	c. 1520
The Exodus	c. 1440
Entry to Canaan	c. 1400
David	c. 1020
Divided Kingdom	c. 940
Northern	
Kingdom falls	727 B.C.
Southern	
Kingdom falls	606-586 B.C.

2. Cyrus (see Isaiah, noted in "Interaction of Some Prophets...") released the first contingent of exiles desiring to return to Jerusalem/Judah. He ruled the Persian Empire until Darius (ruled 521-486 B.C.). Then followed Xerxes (ruled 486-465 B.C.) and Artaxerxes (ruled 465-424 B.C.), in whose court we find Nehemiah.

Babylon falls	539 B.C.
First exiles return	
(Begin rebuilding	
the Temple)	536 B.C.
Complete Temple	516 B.C.
Second exiles	
return	457 B.C.
Nehemiah	
to Jerusalem	444 B.C.

....

Interaction of Some Prophets in the Course of History Surrounding the Exile and the Return from Captivity

Isaiah (c. 740-680 B.C.). Among Isaiah's prophecies was the incredible advance naming of the monarch God would use to liberate the Jews (see Isa. 45).

Jeremiah (events: 626-587 B.C.). Among Jeremiah's prophecies is the specific statement numbering the years of Israel's captivity (see Jer. 25).

Daniel (c. 618-535 B.C.). Daniel lives through the entire captivity. Reading Jeremiah one day, he begins intercession for release (see Dan. 9—10).

Haggai/Zechariah (events 536-516 B.C.). Haggai also lived through the exile and returned. He and Zechariah stirred the people to rebuild the Temple.

Ezra (events c. 536-450 B.C.). As a historian, Ezra records the first return of exiles under Zerubbabel (536 B.C.). As a priest he leads the second contingent (457 B.C.) and is later joined by Nehemiah.

Nehemiah (events c. 444-430 B.C.). Nehemiah is a consultant to Artaxerxes, emperor of the Persian Empire, when as a godly Jewish patriot he asks for release by the king to go assist the condition of the returned exiles. He does so for 12 years.

How Long Was the Project?

The chronology of this book of Nehemiah is complicated and some difference of opinion exists by reason of apparent conflicts in the text. The seeming inconsistencies resolve when simple reasoning is added to one literary practice common to Hebrew literature: the prolepsis.

A "prolepsis" is something written in anticipation of what follows: "The introduction into a narrative of events as taking place before it could have done so, or the treating of a future event as if it had already happened."[1] An example of this is in Nehemiah 3:1, where the walls are described as completed and the doors as having been hung, whereas Nehemiah clearly writes in 6:1 of the doors as not yet being set in place.

A combination of references is helpful in solving the question, How long was the building project in progress?

Some have made the sincere mistake of concluding from Nehemiah 6:15 that the total rebuilding of the walls of Jerusalem took place in 52 days. This is an utter impossibility in view of the complete devastation described in 2:12-15. It is ludicrous to suppose that a task which could be completed in seven to eight weeks would have been neglected for 90 years.

What Nehemiah 6:15 does testify to is the duration of the time between the events in 6:1 and the completion of the hanging of the doors in all the gates. Chapter 6 opens with mention that the gates were all that remained to be finished, and verse 15 indicates that this process was completed in a little more than seven weeks—both a remarkable and reasonable time considering there were 10 great gateways to the city.

We are specifically told by Nehemiah that he served the governorship of the city for a 12-year period (see 5:14), apparently the period of time he requested of Artaxerxes in 2:6. Exactly how much of this time was occupied in the recovery of the walls, until the final placement of the gates, we are never told in a summary statement. But we do know that aside from the delays caused by the resistance of Sanballat and company, the progress was slow enough to cause weariness and discouragement with the massive mounds of rubble (see 4:10).

Make no mistake: Nebuchadnezzar's troops had done their job well 140 years earlier. Jerusalem was ransacked and left as a shame to its people. It was never intended for recovery, and it looked that way.

It is no discrediting of either God's grace among the Jews or Nehemiah's leadership of the project to suggest that it must have taken at the very least, a number of years. Remember, the Temple they were rebuilding had taken 20 years to build.

The idea of the rebuilding of the walls as a 52-day "miracle" (actually 45 days, removing Sabbaths as work days) is not mandated by the text. The grander miracle is displayed in the fact that notwithstanding so much opposition and such complete destruction, the tenacity of the leadership and the people persisted until the shame of nearly a century of neglect was overcome.

Note

1. *Webster's New World Dictionary, Second College Edition.*

APPENDIX C

EXPOSITIONAL APPROACH TO THIS BOOK

The Bible says, "All Scripture is given by inspiration of God, and is profitable for doctrine, for reproof, for correction, for instruction in righteousness, that the man of God may be complete, thoroughly equipped for every good work" (2 Tim. 3:16,17).

This clearly argues against the opinion of some teachers that historical books of the Bible cannot be sources of establishing truth—i.e., doctrine. The New Testament word "doctrine" (*didache*) simply means, "teaching." Most Old Testament historical books contain at least three types of teachings:

1. Facts concerning the past;
2. Moral and spiritual lessons; and
3. Pictures of New Testament truth.

Nehemiah contains all three, and our expositional approach to this book includes an unfolding of a very clear picture of the nature and work of the Holy Spirit assisting the believer in rebuilding life's broken places. This is consistent with the expository style of several New Testament writers and is verified by the clear statements of the Word concerning the content of the Old Testament as it bears on our lives today:

> *For whatever things were written before were written for our learning, that we through the patience and comfort of the Scriptures might have hope (Rom. 15:4).*

> *Now all these things happened to them as examples, and they were written for our admonition, on whom the ends of the ages have come (1 Cor. 10:11).*

Coverage of the book of Nehemiah has not been exhaustive, since the nature of much of its content does not contribute to anything other than historical information. Nehemiah contains 13 chapters and 406 verses: 189 list names, 38 recite earlier history and 179 involve Nehemiah's action. Thus this study, dealing essentially with Nehemiah, his work, leadership and influence, has only elaborated on less than half the book's actual content. Still, little of the essence of its message is left untouched, whether historical, factual, spiritual or typical.

The following outline shows those portions adapted for the present study and makes it obvious why large segments (mostly census and name lists) are omitted.

OUTLINE OF NEHEMIAH

Chapter   Content

1. Nehemiah receives report (vv. 1-3) and prays for Jerusalem (vv. 4-11).
2. Nehemiah appeals to king (vv. 1-8), travels to Jerusalem (vv. 9-11), surveys destruction (vv. 12-16) and meets the leaders (vv. 17-20).
3. Listing of builders (vv. 1-32).
4. Sanballat's tirade (vv. 1-3); Nehemiah's prayer/response (vv. 4-6) and resisting conspiracy (vv. 7-23).
5. Problems governing the people (vv. 1-19).
6. Sanballat's efforts to distract Nehemiah (vv. 1-14) and completion of project (vv. 15-19).
7. Establishing city (vv. 1-5) and Zerubbabel's registry (vv. 6-73).
8. Reading of the Law (vv. 1-12) and observing the Feast (vv. 13-18).
9. Confession, repentance (vv. 1-3) and review of history (vv. 4-38).
10. Covenant to obey Law (vv. 1-39).
11. Dwellers in Jerusalem (vv. 1-36).
12. Dwellers in Jerusalem (vv. 1-26) and dedication of the wall (vv. 27-47).
13. Nehemiah returns and reforms (vv. 1-31).

COVERAGE IN THIS BOOK

NOTES

Chapter 1
1. Romans 12:3.

Chapter 2
1. Nehemiah 1:2.
2. Mark 10:43.
3. Jeremiah 25:11; 29:10.
4. Isaiah 44:28; Ezra 1:1-4.
5. Deuteronomy 6:4; Mark 12:29,30.
6. Ezra 3—6.
7. Ezra 6:15.
8. Nehemiah 1:11.

Chapter 3
1. John 14:17.
2. John 16:14.
3. John 14:16.
4. See Ephesians 5:18,19
5. John 10:7,9; John 14:6; Acts 4:12.
6. John 1:29.
7. John 1:33.
8. Galatians 3:3.
9. Romans 8:1.
10. By William J. Kirkpatrick. Public domain.

Chapter 4
1. Genesis 1:27.
2. John 3:3.
3. 2 Corinthians 5:17, *KJV*.
4. See 1 Corinthians 7:15.

Chapter 5
1. From this reference onward, all italicized words and phrases in Scripture quotation are added by the author for emphasis and clarification.
2. Hebrews 4:12.
3. John 4:24.

4. Nehemiah 1:4.
5. Ephesians 4:17-19.
6. Ezekiel 18:4.
7. Ephesians 2:1-3.
8. 1 Thessalonians 5:23.

Chapter 6
1. Nehemiah 1:4,5.
2. Nehemiah 1:5,11.
3. Nehemiah 1:11,5.
4. Nehemiah 1:7.
5. Nehemiah 1:8.
6. Nehemiah 1:11.
7. See Romans 8:26,27.

Chapter 7
1. 1 Thessalonians 5:23.
2. Leviticus 11:44.
3. Matthew 5:48.
4. 1 John 3:8.
5. 1 John 2:1,2.
6. See Nehemiah 2:5,6.
7. Psalm 138:8.

Chapter 8
1. Matthew 18:3,4.
2. Harry D. Clark, *Into My Heart*. Public domain.
3. See Hebrews 10:17.
4. Romans 5:1, *KJV*.
5. See Luke 15:7.
6. See Luke 10:20.
7. Romans 6:23, *KJV*.
8. See Hebrews 13:5; John 10:10.
9. Romans 8:31,37.
10. 1 Corinthians 3:11.
11. John 3:7.
12. See Ephesians 2:8,9.
13. See Titus 3:5.
14. There is an actual sense in

which we are viewed as holy (sanctified) at the time of our regeneration; but all Scripture notes that this position we are given by faith is intended to summon our growth *into* that gracious acceptance God grants us *while* we are growing.

15. See Philippians 1:6.
16. See Joel 2:23-29.
17. See Exodus 20:2.
18. John 1:29.
19. Nehemiah 2:7.
20. See Matthew 16:17-19.
21. See John 14:13,14, *KJV*.
22. See Nehemiah 2:20.
23. Matthew 28:18.
24. Nehemiah 2:8.
25. Philippians 1:19; 4:19.
26. Philippians 2:13.

Chapter 9
1. Traditional Negro spiritual. Public domain.
2. See Matthew 26:53.
3. See Colossians 2:18.
4. See Acts 12:4-10.
5. See Acts 8:26.
6. See Acts 12:20-23.
7. See Acts 27:23.
8. Hebrews 1:14.
9. Psalm 91:11,12.
10. See 2 Kings 6.
11. Ephesians 6:12.
12. Nehemiah 2:10.
13. See Isaiah 14:12-15; Ezekiel 29:11-19.
14. See Genesis 3; Revelation 12.
15. Matthew 28:18.
16. Ephesians 2:2.
17. See 1 John 5:19.
18. See John 8:44.
19. See Matthew 13:24-30; 36-43.
20. See Luke 8:12.

21. See John 10:10.
22. See Isaiah 59:19.
23. See 1 John 4:4.
24. Philippians 1:6.

Chapter 10
1. See Romans 8:14.
2. See Nehemiah 2:12,13; 15.
3. See Psalm 121:4.
4. Psalm 3:5.
5. See Psalm 138:8.
6. See Jeremiah 32:35
7. See John 8:36.
8. John 4:14.
9. See Isaiah 12:3.

Chapter 11
1. 1 John 1:7.
2. 1 John 1:9.
3. Nehemiah 2:14.
4. John 15:3.
5. Nehemiah 2:14.
6. John 9:7.
7. Acts 2:38.
8. John 4:14.
9. See John 7:38.
10. Acts 2:39.

Chapter 12
1. Nehemiah 2:16.
2. Nehemiah 2:17.
3. John 3:16,17.
4. John 1:14,18.
5. See Romans 8:17.
6. Luke 15:1,2.
7. Luke 15:4-7.
8. Luke 15:8-10.
9. See Hebrews 4:15.
10. Hebrews 4:16.
11. Nehemiah 2:18.
12. Nehemiah 2:18.
13. Nehemiah 2:19.
14. Nehemiah 2:20.

15. See Romans 8:31-33.
16. See Nehemiah 2:20.

Chapter 13

1. Romans 14:7.
2. See 1 John 4:18 and John 8:32.
3. See Ephesians 5:21.
4. 1 Peter 5:5.
5. Romans 12:5.
6. Ephesians 4:16.
7. See John 17:21.
8. See Ephesians 2:22.

Chapter 14

1. See John 10:10.
2. John 10:10.
3. See James 4:7 and 1 Peter 5:9.
4. See Nehemiah 4:1.
5. See Revelation 12:12.
6. See Daniel 7:25.
7. See Revelation 12:12.
8. 1 John 4:4.
9. See 2 Corinthians 12:7-10.
10. Philippians 4:13.
11. Nehemiah 4:10.
12. See Galatians 6:9.
13. Nehemiah 4:2.
14. See Luke 4:18.
15. Luke 4:8.

Chapter 15

1. Nehemiah 4:11.
2. Hebrews 12:1. Read also Hebrews 11.
3. Nehemiah 4:14, *TLB*.
4. Matthew 18:19,20.
5. See Revelation 1:9.
6. See Revelation 12:11.
7. Nehemiah 4:16,18.
8. 1 Peter 5:8.
9. Ephesians 6:10-20.
10. Ephesians 6:16.
11. Proverbs 4:23.

12. Romans 5:1.
13. Luke 10:19.
14. Ephesians 1:21,22.
15. Romans 10:17.
16. 2 Corinthians 10:4,5.
17. James 4:7. See also 1 Peter 5:9.
18. 2 Corinthians 2:11.
19. Nehemiah 4:23.

Chapter 16

1. Nehemiah 5:1.
2. Hebrews 12:29.
3. Isaiah 63:10.
4. Nehemiah 13:4-12,15-21,23-30, *TLB*.
5. See Nehemiah 5:1,2.
6. See Nehemiah 5:3,4.
7. See Nehemiah 5:5.
8. See Nehemiah 13:1-3,23-29.
9. See Nehemiah 13:4-8.
10. See Nehemiah 13:9-13.
11. See Nehemiah 13:15-22.
12. See John 5:14.
13. Luke 11:24-26.
14. John 8:11.

Chapter 17

1. See Mark 13:31.
2. Genesis 1:1.
3. John 1:1.
4. 2 Peter 1:4,8, author paraphrase.
5. Nehemiah 8:10.
6. See 1 Thessalonians 5:24.
7. See Luke 1:37.
8. Philippians 2:13.
9. 2 Corinthians 7:10,11.
10. See Matthew 13:18-23.
11. See Acts 8:8.
12. Psalm 46:10.
13. Isaiah 40:1,2.
14. Psalm 16:11.
15. Philippians 4:4, *KJV*.
16. Nehemiah 8:10.
17. See Luke 2:10,11.

Fan the Flame with These Resources from Jack Hayford

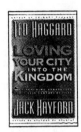

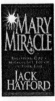

Continuing Education for Church Leaders

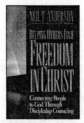
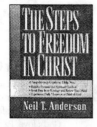

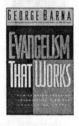

Resources for Cutting Edge Leaders

Setting Your Church Free

Neil T. Anderson and Charles Mylander

Spiritual battles can affect entire churches as well as individuals. *Setting Your Church Free* shows pastors and church leaders how they can apply the powerful principles from *Victory Over the Darkness* to lead their churches to freedom.

Hardcover • ISBN 08307.16556

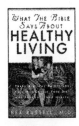

What the Bible Says About Healthy Living

Rex Russell, M.D.

Learn three biblical principles that will help you improve your physical—and spiritual—health. This book gives you practical, workable steps to improve your health and overall quality of life.

Paperback • ISBN 08307.18583

The Healthy Church

C. Peter Wagner

When striving for health and growth of a church, we often overlook things that are killing us. If we can detect and counteract these diseases we can grow a healthy, Christ-directed church.

Hardcover • ISBN 08307.18346

Fasting for Spiritual Breakthrough

Elmer L. Towns

This book gives you the biblical reasons for fasting, and introduces you to nine biblical fasts—each designed for a specific physical and spiritual outcome.

Paperback • ISBN 08307.18397

The Voice of God

Cindy Jacobs

Cut through confusion and see how prophecy can be used in any church. You'll get a clear picture of biblical prophecy and how an individual can exercise this spiritual gift to edify the church.

Paperback • ISBN 08307.17730

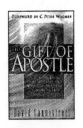

The Gift of Apostle

David Cannistraci

Find out why God has given the Church apostles—leaders with a clear mission to mobilize and unify the church—and see what the Bible says about the apostolic gift for today's church.

Hardcover • ISBN 08307.18451

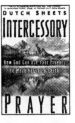

Intercessory Prayer

Dutch Sheets

Find inspiration to reach new levels of prayer, the courage to pray for the "impossible" and the persistence to see your prayers through to completion.

"Of all the books on prayer I have read, none compares to Intercessory Prayer!" –C. Peter Wagner

Hardcover • ISBN 08307.18885

That None Should Perish

Ed Silvoso

Ed Silvoso shows that dramatic things happen when we pray for people. Learn the powerful principles of "prayer evangelism" and how to bring the gospel to your community, reaching your entire city for Christ.

Paperback • ISBN 08307.16904

Ask for these resources at your local Christian bookstore.

Regal
A Division of Gospel Light